IMAGES OF JESUS

*How Jesus Is Perceived and Portrayed
in Non-European Cultures*

ANTON WESSELS

translated by JOHN VRIEND

WILLIAM B. EERDMANS PUBLISHING COMPANY
GRAND RAPIDS, MICHIGAN

The author and publisher acknowledge with gratitude the permission granted by Orbis Books to reprint material from several of their publications cited throughout this volume.

21763739

Originally published as *Jezus zien: hoe Jezus is overgeleverd in andere culturen*
© 1986 by Uitgeverij Ten Have b.v., Baarn, the Netherlands

First English edition copyright © 1990 by Wm. B. Eerdmans Publishing Co.
255 Jefferson Ave. S.E., Grand Rapids, Michigan 49503

Reprinted, October 1991

Library of Congress Cataloging-in-Publication Data

Wessels, Anton.
    [Jezus zien. English]
    Images of Jesus: how Jesus is perceived and portrayed in non-European
cultures / Anton Wessels; translated by John Vriend. — 1st English ed.
        p.   cm.
    Translation of: Jezus zien.
    Includes index.
    ISBN 0-8028-0287-7
    1. Jesus Christ — History of doctrines. I. Title.
BT198.W45513 1990
232'.09 — dc20   90-37067
                                                                        CIP

TO
LAMBRECHT,
GODFRIED,
AND
MARIE-ODILE

About the cover
The Cameroon artist Engelbert Mweng created this image in the apse of a chapel in Douala, Cameroon. In the original version, three colors were used that have special meaning in West Africa: black stands for suffering, white for the dead, and red for the living. "In the semicircular apse he stretches his arms not only upward but also to the fore, so that he encompasses the whole world that he views from the cross" (Weber).

"When the African comes into encounter with Jesus Christ, he welcomes him as the Son of God, as the Lord of the living and the dead, as the one who through life, doctrine, wonders, suffering, death, and resurrection is the greatest initiating teacher, as the one who knows the eternal truth of the doings of life and death, as the one who lives life definitively over death" (Engelbert Mweng).

CONTENTS

INTRODUCTION

Who do men say that the Son of man is?

Matthew 16:13

WHEN in 1939 J. H. Bavinck assumed the position of professor of mission at the Theological School in Kampen and at the Free University in Amsterdam, the Netherlands, his inaugural lecture bore the title "Preaching Christ among the Nations of the World." The subject of this book is similar: How has Jesus been interpreted and his image passed on in Europe and in other than European cultures? From century to century, how was he conveyed, "translated," proclaimed? And how was he received in the contexts in which he "appeared" and was preached?

In order to discover how he was portrayed in other than European cultures, I shall first consider the changing image of Jesus which existed and still exists in Europe. The question which constantly urges itself upon one's attention in this connection is this: In the process of handing down the gospel of Jesus, was he perhaps also somewhat betrayed? Is the translator *(traductor)* in this process possibly at the same time the traitor *(traditor)*? One wonders: Can transmission ever take place without betrayal?

1

The Fish

In the early centuries of the Christian era one encounters no depictions of Jesus Christ. The manner of expression chosen first was symbolic. One of the best-known symbols, found in the catacombs, is that of the fish. The Greek word for fish, *ichthus*, was viewed as an acrostic for *Iēsous Christos Theou Huios Sōtēr*: Jesus Christ, Son of God, Savior. In the illustration above, children had this symbol inscribed on the grave of "their dear parents who are resting here till the resurrection."

THE CHANGING IMAGE OF JESUS IN EUROPE

When asking the question as to which image of Jesus has been passed on from Europe into other cultures, one must be aware how inconstant that image has been and still is in Europe itself. In the process, perspectives repeatedly seem to switch. One way to observe this phenomenon is to look at how Jesus has been reproduced in art. There one sees reflected the faith, the piety, as well as the theological conceptions, of the ages.

Although legends refer to the existence of authentic portraits of Jesus allegedly not made with human hands (*acheiropoeta*), in reality we do not even possess accurate descriptions of how Jesus was said to have looked. In the fifth century A.D. Augustine of Hippo testifies to this when he says that we do not know exactly how he looked.[1]

At the very beginning Jesus was represented symbolically or allegorically, two of the most popular representations in this connection being the fish and the lamb. The alpha and omega (the A and the Ω) were used as the Christ-monogram.

It is likely that in the early centuries, for reasons of security, the sign of the cross remained hidden. Only after the vision of Constantine the Great in A.D. 312—"in that sign you will conquer"—does the sign of the cross occur publicly.

In that symbolic or allegorical representation the significance of Jesus for salvation is emphasized—something also true in many later images. The most ancient representations of Jesus in human form can be found in the catacombs of Rome and in the church of Dura Europos, a town on the right bank of the Euphrates. There Jesus is represented as a youthful-looking "good shepherd," a

---

1. Aurelius Augustine, *The Trinity*, VIII, 4.

figure that in time became very popular. Often he is pictured carrying a male sheep on his shoulders, suggesting Luke 15:5 ("And when he has found it, he lays it on his shoulders, rejoicing") and Psalm 23 ("The Lord is my shepherd"), as well as John 10:11 ("I am the good shepherd. The good shepherd lays down his life for the sheep"). The "good shepherd" who symbolizes Jesus develops in two directions: into the pastoral figure who is also a teacher—for Clement of Alexandria (d. ca. 215) he was an educator and teacher—and into the minstrel-shepherd.

In the latter case, as the captions under the representations indicate, we are dealing with Jesus as the true Orpheus, and he is often depicted with a cither. To Clement of Alexandria the true divine minstrel is not Orpheus but Christ, who introduces a new song into the world. "He at least is the only one who ever tamed the most intractable of all wild beasts—man. . . . And all these most savage beasts, and all such stones, the heavenly song of itself transformed into men of gentleness. . . . See how mighty is the new song! It has made men out of stones and men out of wild beasts. They who were otherwise dead, who had no share in the real and true life, revived when they but heard the song."[2]

Initially this shepherd figure is given a youthful appearance, *Christus iuvenis*, with a round face, still beardless, and short hair. In place of the garments of a shepherd he wears the upper-class clothes of that time, particularly the tunic, pallium (cloak), and sandals, like a young patrician. This Jesus does not so much resemble an Oriental as a Roman. The fact that he is made to look handsome is sometimes said to be for apologetic reasons.

---

2. *Clement of Alexandria*, "Exhortation to the Greeks," G. W. Butterworth, trans., Loeb Classical Library (New York: G. P. Putnam & Sons, 1919), pp. 9, 11. According to Eusebius of Caesarea, Christ cast a spell on recalcitrant sinners as Orpheus did on wild animals.

The Good Shepherd
From the time depictions of Jesus Christ arose, there existed a
clear preference for the figure of the Good Shepherd. A great
many of them date back to the third and fourth centuries. This
depiction from the first half of the third century can be found
in the center medallion of a ceiling fresco of the vault of Lucina,
which is connected with the catacomb of Callixtus in Rome. It
is the figure of a shepherd carrying a sheep on his shoulders:
the symbol of a rescue. "It is always dear to the heart of God
to save the flock of human beings" (Clement of Alexandria,
Proteptikos II, 116, 1).

The modifications or variations which first show up have to do with the age of the One depicted. The face becomes longer; his hair hangs down as far as the shoulders and is parted in the middle. A beard appears. Now the face does assume an Oriental cast and acquires a brown complexion. The images arise of the "exalted Lord," particularly those of the teacher and lawgiver. Sometimes the earthly, itinerant Jesus is depicted without a beard, while the bearded Jesus reproduces the exalted Lord. He is pictured as a thirty-three-year-old adult. It is as such, presumably, that he became known to many people and can be found, for instance, on the famed mosaics in Ravenna, the seat of government of the western Roman Empire for a time, in S. Apollinare Nuova. The mosaics of Ravenna are sometimes regarded as an illustration of the transition from a theophanous Christology, i.e., a Christology in which God *manifests* himself, to a Christology in which God *becomes incarnate.*[3]

Still, the different images of Jesus—with or without a beard; short or long hair—must not be viewed merely as the product of the creative imagination of some artist. Rather, this succession of images says something about the faith of those first centuries, about the attitude of the church from the earliest times of persecution on: "In this figure full of youthful vibrancy and kindness all the ideas which the earliest artists and their contemporaries associated with the person and work of the Son of God and the Son of man became crystallized. Without being conscious of it this age understood itself in and through the younger Christ-ideal."

When the persecutions stopped, the idea of the return of Christ receded; the church became the imperial church and turned its attention toward earth; it had come of age, in

3. H. Corbin, *L'imagination creatrice dans le soufisme d'ibn Arabi* (Paris: Flammarion, 1958), p. 276.

the sense of male adulthood."[4] The victory of Constantine the Great signified the victory of Christianity over paganism, a conquest and victory mirrored in the art of the time. Images of Jesus arose which were derived from the emperor worship of late antiquity, and which symbolized Christ's triumph: *Christus Victor,* crowned by the hand of God, the world-ruler, Pantokrator.

In the Middle Ages the humanity or humanness of Jesus began to be strongly emphasized. Toward A.D. 1000 the first sculpted forms of the crucifix made their appearance, as, for example, the "Gero-cross" in Cologne. In Romanesque cathedrals Christ is depicted as God who has assumed human form. Worshipers in the first half of the twelfth century who entered the cathedrals of Beaulieu, Autun, or Vezelay were welcomed on the threshold by Christ as a terrifying world Judge. In a related image, one thinks of Christ as the wrathful Judge of the living and the dead whom Michelangelo painted above the altar of the Sistine chapel. Although in the Gothic period of the thirteenth century Jesus was increasingly depicted as an earthly being, the theme of his being "king" and "conqueror" was still maintained. In the High Gothic era the sculptures lost their supra-mundane severity and gained the features of noble humanity, as evidenced in the cathedrals of Chartres and Amiens. With reference to the representation of Christ in the narthex of the cathedral of Chartres people speak of his distinguished aristocratic

---

4. For this entire section, cf. "Christusbilder," in *Realencyclopedie für protestantische Theologie und Kirche,* vol. 4, pp. 73-77; further, F. van der Meer, *Images du Christ dans la sculture au nord des Alpes et des Pyrénées* (Antwerp and Paris: Fonds Mercator/Albin Michel, 1980); R. Koning, "Christus in de schilderkunst en beeldhouwkunst" in *Christus de Heiland,* F. Grosheide, ed. (Kampen: Kok, 1948), pp. 243-82; H. A. Stützer, *Die Kunst der römischen Katacomben* (Cologne: DuMont Buchverlag, 1983), esp. pp. 37, 44, 45.

The Suffering Christ
The Brazilian sculptor Guido Rocha depicted his own experience
of torture (and that of others) in this sculpture of the tortured
Christ. "As he himself uttered a cry of pain, Rocha remembered
the Christ who cried out on the cross, and this Golgotha-cry
became for him *the* great promise: here was a human being who,
while enduring the fiercest torments, still remained fully human;
who fulfilled his mission of love; who was a human being for his
fellow humans right into the hour of truth. There was no break
between his message and his life and death. Accordingly, to this
Brazilian artist the barely tolerable face of the dying Christ,
seemingly possessed by demonic spirits, is not an image of
aversion and revulsion, but a sign of hope." (Translated from the
Dutch; source not indicated.—TRANS.)

bearing, which had taken the place of a kind of ascetic sublimity.

Under the influence of St. Bernard of Clairvaux and St. Francis of Assisi it was the earthly Jesus in his suffering who captured the attention of the devout: the Christ triumphant became a long-suffering Christ *(Christus patiens)*. The late Middle Ages were dominated by death and associated themes. In the foreground is the attainment of personal salvation: the suffering Christ who brings "perfect righteousness" also calls to "imitate" him, the Man of Sorrows, who in his suffering became like us. In this period, the so-called *Andachtsbilder* (devotional sculptures) appear on altars to call the devout to conformity with his suffering and to mystical union with him.

The oldest example of a "pietà" comes down from the thirteenth century. But here, in the words of R. Koning, the body has become a hideous lump of misery: "thick tangles of clotted blood adhere to his wounds, while his arms and legs hang limp. The head, with eyes closed and mouth slightly open, the last breath just having escaped, falls over backward. . . . Mary in her grief blends in with this. Thus originated a statue of concentrated sorrow and deep gloom. The effect is one of ghastly realism which in its starkness has become a totally shattering cry." But in the "pietà" which Michelangelo sculptured—at least the one which is currently on display at St. Peter's in Rome—Christ has become the prototype of the ideal "renaissance" man: "In his perfection the natural is crowned and the transcendent becomes visible. To this naturalistic idealism the divinity of the Redeemer manifests itself in a corporeality raised to the level of classic beauty."

In the fifteenth century Jesus is portrayed as a man existing in the historical environment of the artist, in Flanders, for instance. Pieter Brueghel "The Elder" (ca. 1525/30–69) localizes Jesus' crossbearing in his own time (1564) and milieu: "The sacrifice of Golgotha is something which concerns the people of all times and places, also Flanders where he paints it." On the Isenheim altar at Colmar, Matthias Grünewald depicted, in a deeply moving and shocking manner, a hideously tortured man on a cross (finished ca. 1516), which especially today calls to mind the contemporary Latin American counterparts, where in numerous instances the tortured are pictured hanging on a cross.

In Matthias Grünewald's representation, John the Baptist's (overly) long finger points to the One who must increase even as he must decrease (John 3:30). One cannot help noticing how far removed this painting is from the time of the Apollo-like beauty of the "good shepherd" when the "man of sorrows" is depicted very realistically. In the representation of the Trinity (Vienna), the Crucified can be seen in the midst of the opened mantle of God the Father: he "whom God put forward as an expiation by his blood, to be received by faith" (Rom. 3:25). From the perspective of the Middle Ages it is very revolutionary when Albrecht Dürer, in a self-portrait, depicts himself as the man of sorrows, an act in which the "Christ-image" and "the human-image" are apparently interchangeable.

The highest degree of spiritualization is attained in the art of El Greco, whose paintings reflect the influence of the mysticism of St. John of the Cross and Theresa of Avila. Velázquez, "the master of Spanish Baroque," also introduces themes borrowed from mysticism: "He charms both the mind and the sense in a manner similar to the dominant principle of Ignatius of Loyola." The distinguishing features of the baroque Christ-image were the qualities of the emotional and the visionary. It is these baroque images and sculptures in particular which in time become important for the "transmission" of Jesus to the newly "discovered" worlds at which the church's mission was aimed. Certain sculptures in Japan, as well as the so-called "santos" (life-

The Last Supper
Armenia is the most ancient Christian kingdom, now one of
the republics of the Soviet Union. This representation of the
Last Supper was made in 1720. Among other things it shows
Jesus giving a morsel to Judas. The tile is located in the Etch-
miadzin chapel in Jerusalem.

size wooden figures) in New Mexico, provide the link between the themes of suffering in the Spanish Baroque and
the creations which appeal to native tradition.

The Christ-images of Peter Paul Rubens, sometimes
called the painter of the Counter-Reformation, portray
Spanish piety and the triumph of Christ's church. Even in
suffering Christ summons people to a heroic attitude. In the
Protestant tradition one must of course think especially of the
many renderings of Christ painted and drawn by Rembrandt.

The Christ who extends his hands in blessing and
carries a lamb on his shoulders originated in the nineteenth
century (ca. 1822), and was the work of the Danish artist
Bertel Thorwaldsen. This Christ adorned the living rooms
of numerous Protestant homes far into the twentieth century and, for that matter, many homes and churches in Africa!
It is worth noting that in his day Søren Kierkegaard criti-
cized that picture because the offense of the cross had been
eliminated from it.

Vincent van Gogh's "The Resurrection of Lazarus"
(1890; after Rembrandt) does not depict Christ himself, but,
as was done early in the history of the church, represents
him symbolically. Here again, as then, the significance of
Jesus Christ for salvation is brought out: hence the aura of
light around Lazarus and his sisters.

It can be said of different periods that it was "the goal
of art to interpret the redemptive work of Christ."[5] In

5. For this overview, see *Die Religion in Geschichte und Gegenwart*,
3d ed., s.v. "Christusbild" (Tübingen: Mohr, 1957); Koning, pp. 249, 251,
252, 256, 275, 277; cf. also J. Cobb, *Christ in a Pluralistic Age* (Philadelphia:
Westminster, 1975); A. Malraux, *The Voices of Silence* (New York: Doubleday, 1960); W. A. Visser 't Hooft, *Rembrandt and the Gospel* (London:
SCM, 1957).

For depictions of the suffering Christ in Latin America and other
places, cf. H. R. Weber, *On a Friday Noon: Meditations Under the Cross*
(Grand Rapids: Eerdmans, 1979).

For examples of Thorwaldsen's representation of Jesus in Africa, cf.

European art Jesus is depicted right into the twentieth century. He is reproduced in numerous variations—for example, by the painter Georges Rouault, inter alia, in his "Man of Sorrows" of 1932. In the introduction to his book *Images du Christ* F. van der Meer writes that today in the art of sculpture there is hardly any room left for Christ. He then continues: "It is not surprising: this absence is also an interior absence. The person who no longer believes in the appearance of the uncreated Wisdom of God gradually loses all interest in the mysterious man that Jesus was. The eyes of the man born blind only opened when the man believed in the existence of one he had not known before."[6]

PORTRAYAL OR BETRAYAL?

From this very sketchy, necessarily limited survey at least this much has become clear: different theological perspectives and emphases from distinct periods and regions are mirrored in the changing images of Jesus in Europe as depicted in art. But both here and in the sequel to this book we cannot help asking whether we are dealing with so many

---

O. Sander, "Jesus Christus in Bekenntnis Afrikanischer Kirchen," *Zeitschrift für Mission* 1 (1975): 71; R. W. Taylor, *Jesus in Indian Paintings* (Madras: Christian Literature Society for India, 1975), p. 39, refers to J. Jennes, "De Uitstraling van de Vlaamse Prenthunst in Indie, China, en Japan Tijdens de XVI efen XVIIe Eeuw, Enkele Nieuwe Gegevens," in *Miscellanea Jozef Duverger* (Gent: Uitgave Vereniging voor de geschiedenis der textielkunsten, 1968), p. 479; D. Johnson Fleming, *Each with His Own Brush; Contemporary Christian Art in Asia and Africa* (New York: Friendship Press, 1938): "As at Pentecost, Parthians, Medes and Elamites heard the message, 'every man in his own tongue wherein he was born,' so we see Chinese and Japanese and Indians expressing Christianity's universal language, each with his own brush" (p. 1).
    6. Van der Meer, p. 79.

legitimate representations of Jesus Christ and facets of his work and significance, or whether at times or even more frequently he is misrepresented, caricatured, or even betrayed.

It is striking that in the New Testament the apostolic task is described with the word: "to hand over to another" *(paradidōmi)*. In Greek as in English this can mean different things. It can mean "to hand down by tradition," but it can also mean "to deliver up or surrender," in the sense of betrayal. In Paul's letter to the Corinthians the word occurs in both meanings in the same context: "For I received from the Lord what I also *delivered* to you, that the Lord Jesus on the night when he was *betrayed* took bread . . ." (1 Cor. 11:23). Obviously an apostle can be or become "one who hands over," even in the sense of Judas the betrayer.

The question we raise in this book is whether the apostles, and later the churches and the missionaries, faithfully transmitted and preached that which they saw and heard (cf. 1 John 1:1-3), or whether they betrayed Jesus and his message. The question needs to be posed already with regard to the "transmission" of Jesus in all those centuries of European history. Was it a "handing over" in the sense of betrayal when Jesus was apparently represented as a Ruler from whom church and state derived their authority? Was the conversion of Constantine to the Christian church not one of the ways by which he sought to integrate the Roman Empire? The Byzantine representation of Christ as Pantokrator can as such be viewed as a depiction of the words of Matthew 28:18: "All authority in heaven and on earth has been given to me." But one must ask whether the post-Constantinian interpretation of these words makes the confession that "Jesus is Lord" *(Iesos Christos Kurios)* sound as if he were a kind of Caesar who legitimates the power of the Christian emperor. Does not the emperor, under the interpretation of Eusebius, become the symbol of the victorious

Pantokrator

Numerous times Christ has been depicted as the Pantokrator, "the ruler over all." These representations of the enthroned and ruling Christ can be found especially in the domes and apses of churches of the Byzantine tradition. This representation originated in the monastery of St. Neophytos (12th century) on Cyprus. While Christos Pantokrator is found as a rule in an apse, this one was fixed at eye level in a chapel.

Christ,[7] and from the fourth century on do we not see
enacted what G. J. Heering called *The Fall of Christianity*[8]
Does this not create a great distance between the Jesus of the
gospels, the One who proclaimed the gospel to the poor, and
this Jesus of Constantinian triumph? Who actually won—
Jesus Christ or the emperor? Did people not forget that the
nub of the original confession "Jesus Christ is Lord" was
that the Lord *(kurios)* became a servant *(doulos)*, and as
servant-Lord he both has all authority in heaven and on
earth and will be with his disciples to the close of the age?

The Taiwanese theologian Choan-Seng Song points out
how the *pax Romana* was replaced by the *pax Christiana* and
how Jesus, rather than being presented as the friend of all—in
particular of the poor and humiliated—was pictured as
emperor and lawgiver, judge, philosopher, cosmic lord, and
ruler of all things. And thus, as can be illustrated from art, the
humble stable becomes a royal palace and the holy virgin and
the good Joseph are changed into members of the royal court.[9]

The later "colonial Christ," as he was transmitted from
the fifteenth century on from Europe to Africa, the Americas, and Asia—is he not a figure more in keeping with the
"fall" of Christianity? Has it not frequently happened that
people ventured forth not so much to serve as to rule? Is that
not the story of what the Spanish and Portuguese in particular did, followed by other Europeans?

The planting of the first cross on Philippine soil is
depicted in a painting by Vicente Manansala. Here the artist
clearly shows the link between "mission" and "imperial-
ism." A priest blesses a large cross which has just been

7. Cf. D. Savramis, *Jezus overleeft zijn moordenaars* (Baarn: Ten Have,
1974), p. 63.

8. G. J. Heering, *The Fall of Christianity* (New York: Garland Publishing, 1972).

9. Choan-Seng Song, *Third-Eye Theology: Theology in Formation in
Asian Settings* (Maryknoll, NY: Orbis, 1979), pp. 9, 12.

planted by indigenous laborers, while Spanish soldiers carrying spears bark orders at them.[10]

We are forced to ask whether, then as well as later, the message of Jesus and therefore his image was not thus turned into its opposite: the cross as a sign of the execution of an innocent victim having been turned around to function as a sword that could be used against Jews (culminating in the Holocaust), Muslims (the Crusades), redskinned Indians (Indian wars), and blacks (slave trade and slavery).

If one should ask who Judas is in Leonardo da Vinci's *Last Supper*, then, unless one gets special help in identifying him, it will prove a difficult question to answer. Other representations of this scene are very different. There Judas has been conspicuously set apart from the others around the table—the answer is easy. Da Vinci painted the moment at which Jesus said: "One of you will betray me." At that moment *all* the disciples answer: "Is it I, Lord?" (Matt. 26:22). Evidently all the apostles, "traditores" as they are by definition, consider themselves potential "traitors." From the beginning the processes of "handing down" and that of "betrayal" have been bedfellows.

One has to acknowledge the miracle that despite so much betrayal Jesus Christ was nevertheless "passed on"; and let us ask the question: does the transmission of Christ really ever occur without (a degree of) betrayal?

THE PLAN OF THIS BOOK

In the process of examining which image of Jesus has been transmitted, proclaimed, translated, or betrayed in cultures

10. Amarao Takenaka, *Christian Art in Asia* (Tokyo: Kyo Bun Kwan, in association with the Christian Conference of Asia, 1975), p. 18, cf. figure 97.

other than the European—especially since the European
voyages of exploration of the fifteenth century—we are
concerned both with the question which image of Jesus the
bearers of the Christian message brought to other continents
and with the manner in which Jesus was received, understood, or discovered.

Anyone reflecting on the question as to how Jesus was
transmitted in other cultures, i.e., how he crossed all kinds
of boundaries, must be conscious first of all of the fact that
Jesus was a Jew. The question of how Jesus has been, and
is to be, understood in his own Jewish context is of fundamental importance for a Christian regardless of her culture. Available to us are several important contributions by
Jews who are today trying to bring Jesus back home *(Heimhohlung Jesu)*, the Jesus who in so many respects has been
alienated from his own original Jewish background
(chap. 1).

Jesus is not unknown in the Islamic world. It is important to realize that his name is familiar—also apart from
Christian influence—in large parts of the Islamic world via
the image of "the Christ of the Muslims" (chap. 2).

Voyages of "exploration" started in the fifteenth century. Africa was visited, some parts of it for the first time,
and what would later be called Latin America was "visited,"
as it were, by Jesus Christ. Which Jesus is it who was carried
to the New World, that of the Indians, and how was he
received there? What relationship did the Spanish Christ
bear to "Jesus as Liberator"? (chap. 3).

In the same period Europeans penetrated "the black
continent." The slave trade having begun, black Africans
were shipped to the New World. How was Jesus understood
in the African context? Was he "black"? How did the Jesus
who was mediated by European missionaries relate to the
Kwakoe in Suriname?—also an interesting question be-

cause so many of these "African Christians" live as Surinamese people in the Netherlands (chap. 4).

Jesus himself came from Asia, but what is his Asiatic
face (chap. 5)? This question also concerns Jesus' relationship to the great Asiatic religions: Hinduism, Buddhism,
and Taoism. How did Christ walk along the Indian road?—
to allude to the title of the book *(Christ of the Indian Road)* by
the well-known evangelist E. Stanley Jones. And what is
Jesus' relation to the world of Taoism?

Clearly, each chapter deals with an enormous subject
in its own right. Full treatment is out of the question. Still,
we hope to have gathered together enough material from
the three continents of Latin America, Africa, and Asia to be
able to give something of an answer to the question: "But
who do you say that I am?" (Matt. 16:15) (chap. 6).

At Caesarea Philippi Jesus asks his disciples: "Who do
men say that the Son of man is?" All sorts of answers are
given, ranging from John the Baptist redivivus, or Elijah, to
Jeremiah or one of the other prophets. Then comes Jesus'
question: "But who do you say that I am?" From Peter
comes the answer: "You are the Christ, the Son of the living
God" (Matt. 16:13-16).

The same story tells us that Peter, who is pronounced
blessed by Jesus on account of that confession, takes offense
at Jesus because of his statement that he (Jesus) must suffer.
"Get behind me, Satan!" (Matt. 16:23). Some time later Peter
will deny him three times (26:69-75).

Who is Jesus? At the end of his long study of the history
of research in the life of Jesus Albert Schweitzer gives this
answer: "He comes to us as One unknown, without a name,
as of old, by the lake side, He came to those men who knew
Him not. He speaks to us the same word: 'Follow thou me!'
and sets us to the tasks which He has to fulfil for our time.
He commands. And to those who obey Him, whether they

be wise or simple, He will reveal Himself in the toils, the
conflicts, the sufferings which they shall pass through in His
fellowship, and, as an ineffable mystery, they shall learn in
their own experience who He is."[11]

11. A. Schweitzer, *The Quest of the Historical Jesus* (London: Adam
and Charles Black, 1911), p. 401.

I   JESUS: A JEW

> *Whoever has Jesus Christ in faith cannot wish not to have*
> *the Jews. He must have them along with Jesus Christ as his*
> *ancestors and kinsmen. Otherwise he cannot have even the*
> *Jew Jesus. Otherwise with the Jews he rejects Jesus Himself.*
>
> Karl Barth

IN this chapter I shall venture to look at the Jewish understanding of Jesus. I shall begin by discussing the "appro-
priation" of Jesus by Christians, a process by which he has
been stripped of his Jewishness, and proceed to consider
first the ancient Jewish image of Jesus (Jesus in the Talmud)
and then the modern image (Klausner, Buber). Finally, I
shall discuss the permanent(?) schism between the church
and the synagogue, including how it relates to their respec-
tive understandings of Jesus.

"Jesus was not a Christian but a Jew," said Wellhausen
in a familiar and much-quoted passage.[1] It is really a simple
and self-evident statement, although one cannot say that
Christians have always adequately understood its full im-
port. This utterance pulls Christians up short and confronts

---

1. Julius Wellhausen, *Einleitung in die Drei Ersten Evangelien*, 2d ed.
(Berlin: Reimar, 1911), p. 102.

them with the fact that they have often thought they could
appropriate Jesus for themselves as though they were acquainted with everything there is to know about him. They
forget that, as Jesus said in the familiar statements to the
woman at the well, "salvation is from the Jews" (John 4:22).

"Christians have torn Jesus from the soil of Israel. They
have de-Judaized, uprooted, alienated, Hellenized, and
Europeanized him."[2] One can even say that he was sometimes interpreted in an anti-Jewish way. However, to the
reader of the gospels it is clear that the message of Jesus is
directed in the first place, if not almost exclusively, to Jews.
Jesus' field of labor was largely limited to Galilee and
Jerusalem. Reference is made only a few times to contacts
with non-Jews and the narrative mentions only the occasional
visit outside the territory of Israel. And on such an occasion
Jesus says he has been sent only to the lost sheep of the house
of Israel (Matt. 15:24). At the same time the gospels and the
New Testament as a whole point out to us the fact that beside
the Jews who believe in him and accept him as the "Christ,
the Son of the living God"—to use Peter's confession (Matt.
16:16)—or who, as in the case of Thomas, call him "My Lord
and my God" (John 20:28), there are many who do not believe
in him. In his letter to the Romans Paul speaks in a very
moving way of his "sorrow and unceasing anguish" over this
continuing nonacceptance of Jesus by many Jews (Rom. 9:2).

In the New Testament era the ways of Christians (both
Jewish and Gentile) and Jews do not yet totally diverge.
Church and synagogue still have links. Still, as recent New
Testament scholarship has established rather conclusively,
something of the break between church and synagogue
which historically took place later is mirrored, as it were, in
the account given of Jesus' own attitude toward the Jews.

2. Clemens Thoma, *A Christian Theology of Judaism* (New York:
Paulist Press, 1980), p. 107.

A further occasion for the deep schism between Jews and Christians has been a certain interpretation of the New Testament, e.g., of a number of texts in the Gospel of John or a text like "His blood be on us and on our children!" (Matt. 27:25). Through "Christian" history there runs a bloody trail of persecution of Jews.

The question how things could ever come to this point remains a mystery. To think that the symbol of the cross could be turned into one of the destruction of others, and that (as an American Jew has put it[3]) even the name of Jesus Christ immediately brings up in the minds of Jews the association of pogroms! But one must at least look for an explanation—not an excuse—in the kind of theology or ideology held by the church.

According to Christians, Jews were blind and their minds hardened; when they read Moses they had a veil over their face so that they could not see what they ought to have seen (2 Cor. 3:14-16). Numerous times this point of view was externalized—made visible in churches and cathedrals for the instruction of every Christian. One example among many is the cathedral of Strasbourg, where a triumphant proud church is depicted next to a blindfolded synagogue.[4] In the so-called "passion-window" of the cathedral of Chartres (built between 1215–1240), the devil shoots an arrow into the eye of the synagogue. The result is a condition of permanent blindness in the place of the veil which could at least be removed![5] Jews have been regarded throughout the centuries as "enemies of the cross," and for that reason were persecuted unless they converted to Christianity.

3. Quoted by B. Knappert and H. Starck, *Umkehr und Erneuerung: Erläuterungen zum Synodalbeschluss der Rheinischen Landessynode 1980. Zur Erneuerung des Verhältnisses von Christen und Juden* (Neukirchen: Neukirchener Verlag, 1980), pp. 141, 166.

4. Cf. W. Seiferth, *Synagoge und Kirche im Mittelalter* (Munich: Kösel-Verlag, 1964).

5. Seiferth, p. 144; cf. figure 20.

In the early centuries of the Christian era (but also later), Christians expected that the chosen people—the bearers of the promises, after all—would be the first to see that those promises had begun to be fulfilled in Jesus. For both Jewish and Gentile Christians it was hard to accept the refusal of the overwhelming majority of Jews to acknowledge Jesus as the Messiah, for by this refusal the truth of the Christian faith and the claims embodied in it were subjected to doubt.[6]

In the year 1095, Pope Urban II summoned people to what was to be the first crusade. The object was to liberate the Holy Land, Palestine, from the Muslims (also viewed as "enemies of the cross"). It was then virtually a matter of simple logic for the crusaders on their way to the Holy Land to begin by wiping out a large number of those other "enemies of the cross," the Jews. They killed those Christ-murderers or even God-murderers, as the Jews were called, in among other places, the Rhineland. Hatred of the Jews, both preached and practiced in doctrine, proclamation, and popular piety, thoroughly poisoned the atmosphere, we are told, of communities in which Jews and Christians lived together. Roman Catholic churches practiced a Good Friday custom of bringing a Jew into the worship service (for an honorarium!), and boxing him about the ears to avenge the disgrace of Golgotha.[7] As late as the turn of this century, still in certain Alsatian villages a funeral pyre was erected on the square and a Jew was burned in effigy.[8]

For centuries the church regarded it as its task to

6. J. Maier, *Jesus von Nazareth in der talmudischen Uberlieferung* (Darmstadt: Klissenschaftliche Buchgesellschaft, 1978), p. 2.

7. P. G. Aring, *Christlichen Judenmission; Ihre Geschichte und Problematik dargestellt und untersucht am Beispiel des evangelischen Rheinlandes* (Neukirchen: Neukirchener Verlag, 1980), pp. 20, 21, n.55.

8. Jean Toulat, "Juifs et Chrétiens; Mieux inventorier le patrimoine commun," *Le Monde*, 6 April 1985.

convert Jews. People hoped and prayed and worked for the removal of the "veil." A pastoral letter sent out as late as 1941 by the Dutch Reformed Synod of the Netherlands made this claim: "A Jew is a person of Israel who rejects Jesus Christ. In this respect the Jews are to us *a sign of human hostility against the gospel*. . . . The Jew remains a Jew in the intensely problematic sense which this has first of all for himself: the Jew cannot detach himself from himself as long as he does not come to Christ. . . . The church of Jesus Christ sees itself obligated to pray for the Jews. And, on the basis of ancient but still valid promises, it calls them to the Messiah of the church."[9]

THE JEWS AND JESUS

For a Christian it is a wholesome thing to realize that to the Jews Christianity was not and is not as much an "existential" problem as he or she perhaps thinks. In the early centuries of the church the events involving Jesus under Pontius Pilate did not dominate Jewish consciousness. Rabbinical interest in early Christianity was considerably less than is often thought. Even in the fourth century the Jews regarded paganism, not Christianity, as their worst enemy, a perspective that began to change only as a result of political developments under the oppressive influence of Byzantine (Eastern Roman) religious policies. The Jews regarded the Byzantine-Christian world-power as the fourth empire referred to by Daniel and, according to them, it assumed the character of idolatry.[10]

9. L. de Jong, *Het koninkrijk der Nederlanden in de Tweede Wereldoorlog*, vol. 5, 2d pt. (The Hague: Staatsuitgeverij, 1974), p. 671.
10. Maier, pp. 9, 14, 15, 273, 274.

JESUS IN THE TALMUD

Until the end of the second century, according to David
Flusser, nothing is said in rabbinical sources against the
person of Jesus. Only exorcism in his name is repudiated.[11]
From the end of the second century, polemical statements
against articles in the Christian creed —such as the idea that
God should have a son—begin to appear in rabbinical
literature. Flusser concludes that these instances do not
indicate a Jewish attack on Jesus or on Jewish Christians
because of their faith. Instead, opposition to Jewish Christians arises especially on the social and national level.[12] The
formation of the negative Jewish image of Jesus of the time
has to do with a political constellation. One must be aware
of the reasons for this negative Jewish image of Jesus. In this
climate originated what has sometimes been called "the
gospel of the ghetto." In such a hostile political climate the
rabbinical figure of Ben Pandéra arose, a mock figure who
is presented as the founder of the Christianity which se-
duces people into idolatry.[13]

The *Toledoth Yeshua* are collected stories on the life of
Jesus told by Jews in the form of a parody on the existing
canonical gospels. The story begins as follows: In the time
of the second temple, the time of Emperor Tiberius and of
King Herod II, the wicked king of Jerusalem, there is a man
of the house of David called Joseph ben Pandéra who has a
wife called Mary. His wicked neighbor Yohanan desires to
sleep with Mary, who is beautiful. The narrative continues
by relating how Mary becomes the mother of a bastard son,

11. David Flusser, *Tussen oorsprong en schisma. Artikelen over Jezus,
het jodendom en het vroege christendom* (Hilversum: B. Folkertsma Strehling
voor Talmudica, 1984), pp. 320, 321.

12. Flusser, 1984, p. 321, with reference to G. Aleon, *The Jews in their
Land in the Talmudic Age*, vol. 1 (Jerusalem: Magnus Press, 1980), pp. 305-7.

13. Maier, p. 274.

a sorcerer, idolater, and deceiver, who tries to have himself recognized as son of God. Yeshuh, the miracle-worker, is in the end hanged and deposited on a garbage dump.

The motive for the composition of this "gospel of the ghetto" is to oppose any possible temptation for a Jew to convert to Christianity.[14] This procedure shows a striking resemblance with the apologetic motives which drove people in the Christian Middle Ages to write a polemical biography of the prophet Mohammed, again for the express purpose of preventing Christians from becoming Muslims.[15] Such a profile, of course, has no historical value in the sense that it conveys anything about the real Jesus of history; but it does reveal how at a given time the Jews reacted to the Christian view or image of Jesus.[16]

THE MODERN JEWISH IMAGE OF JESUS

It is extremely interesting, but also very profitable and instructive, for Christians to take note of contemporary Jewish contributions to our understanding of the life and message of Jesus.[17] The object here is very different from that of the earlier polemics mentioned above, for we are now dealing with studies whose goal is to tie in closely with a Jewish understanding of the New Testament and particularly the gospels.[18]

14. J. P. Osier, *L'evangile du Ghetto: la Légende juive de Jésus du II e du xe siede; textes choisis* (Paris: Berg International, 1984); cf. *Le Monde,* 7 December 1984.

15. Cf. N. Daniel, *Islam and the West; The Making of an Image* (Edinburgh: University Press, 1960), chap. 3.

16. Maier, p. 37.

17. Cf. Thoma, p. 166.

18. For research into the understanding of Jesus and the earliest forms of Christianity cf., inter alia, D. Flusser, *Jesus* (New York: Herder and Herder, 1969); *De Joodse oorsprong van het christendom* (Amsterdam, 1964).

This is not to make any sweeping judgment as to the representativeness of these Jewish opinions and views. Still, it is important to mention them. Pinchas Lapide has noted that since the founding of the State of Israel in 1948 more books have been written by Jewish authors about Jesus than in the preceding eighteen centuries. In the present century Joseph Klausner's book *Jesus of Nazareth*[19] has been called the first of the modern Hebrew "lives of Jesus" which used material from the Talmud and Midrash.[20] According to Klausner, Jesus was a Jew, even more Jewish than Hillel, and he remained a Jew till his last breath. It was Jesus' aim to implant in Israel the idea of the coming of the Messiah and to hasten the "end."

However, Jesus sacrificed national life on the altar of an extremely one-sided ethic. Nothing is more dangerous to national Judaism, according to Klausner, than this *exaggerated* Judaism. For it is the ruin of national life and culture when, instead of a call to enact and enforce laws, to implement justice, and to exercise the power of a national state, only belief in God and the practice of an extreme and one-sided ethic in themselves are considered enough. There we have the negation of national life and of the national state. Jesus gave up the God of righteousness and justice in favor of a God of mercy: he sacrificed the God of the social order, the God of the nation, the God of history. However lofty a conception of God Jesus' teachings may represent for the individual moral conscience, it stands for ruin and catastrophe for the public, social, and national conscience. Judaism is not only religion: it is the sum total of everything a nation needs, established on a religious basis. Jesus' over-

19. Joseph Klausner, *Jesus of Nazareth: His Life, Times, and Teaching* (New York, 1925), esp. pp. 369-97; cf. *From Jesus to Paul* (New York, 1943).

20. L. Gillet, *Communion in the Messiah; Studies in the Relationship Between Judaism and Christianity* (London: Redhill Lutterworth Library, 1942), p. 37.

emphasis on self-denial was not Judaism. Klausner refers to
a twofold misapprehension: the nearness of the kingdom
and of his messiahship.[21]

To the Jewish people Jesus is a great moral teacher,
says Klausner, but his extremistic ethical code is a future
dream only for the isolated few, an ideal for the end of the
world and the days of the messiah. It did nothing to
strengthen the national life of Israel. It is not a code for the
nations of today. Still, "in this ethical code there is a sublimity, distinctiveness and originality" unparalleled in any
other Hebrew code; "neither", says Klausner, "is there any
parallel to the remarkable art of his parables. . . . Stripped
of its wrappings of miracles and mysticism" the ethics of
Jesus is "one of the choicest treasures in the literature of
Israel for all time."[22]

Earlier the work of Claude G. Montefiori on the synoptic gospels already had appeared.[23] He views himself as
the first among Jewish scholars to undertake such a modern
inquiry into the life of Jesus. Jesus, at least in his early
preaching, can be described, says Montefiori, as a true
successor to the great pre-exilic prophets Amos, Hosea, and
Isaiah. He sees in Jesus' preaching a revival of prophetic
Judaism. But, says he, the Jew does reject all "Christology"
and has always found his way to the divine Father directly
and without a mediator.[24]

According to Montefiori, Jesus deviates from Jewish
tradition at three points and in that sense is original: in his
concern for sinners; in the posture of life which is marked
by service; and in his love for the poor, the sick, and the
persecuted. In distinction from Klausner, he does not call

21. Reproduced from Gillet's summary, p. 37.
22. Klausner, p. 414.
23. C. G. Montefiori, *The Synoptic Gospels* (London: Macmillan,
1927[2]).
24. Montefiori, chap. 8.

Jesus un-Jewish but hyper-Jewish, because he follows the love-command of the Torah with such extreme radicalism and consistency.[25]

In works which have appeared in the last decades—of which we can mention only a few—the goal is often a kind of rediscovery of Jesus as Jew, a process sometimes called the *Heimhohlung Jesu.* "Who then can separate him from the Jewish people if, as Max Norday (an associate of Theodore Herzl) has said, he is the soul of our soul and the flesh of our flesh?" asks Schalom ben Chorin.[26]

It was the well-known Franz Rosenzweig who remarked that Jesus was especially important for the nations (*goyim*) and was for them the way to the Father, whereas the Jews are already with the Father.[27] Pinchas Lapide, who cites this remark, says that Jesus became exactly what Simeon in Luke 2:32 prophesied he would be: "a light for revelation to the Gentiles, and for glory to thy people Israel." He then refers to the hymn ascribed to Ambrose, *Veni Redemptor gentium,* translated by Luther with *Nun kommt der Heiden Heiland,* Jesus the Savior of the Gentiles. Lapide obviously agrees with that expression.[28]

THE SCHISM

"Quite contrary to his intentions, Jesus became the cause of the schism between Jews and Christians. The hope of Chris-

25. Cf. L. Gillet, p. 37.

26. Schalom ben Chorin, *Bruder Jesu; Der Nazarener in jüdischer Sicht* (Munich: List, 1967), p. 11.

27. F. Rosenzweig, *Briefe,* pub. Edith Rosenzweig (Berlin: Schocken-Verlag, 1935), pp. 73ff.

28. P. Lapide, *Er predigte in ihren Synagogen* (Gütersloh: Gütersloher Verlaghaus Gerd Mohn, 1980), p. 32. Klausner: "From the standpoint of general humanity he is, indeed, 'a light to the Gentiles' " (p. 413).

tianity lies in concentrated attention to Jesus' own message. Then Jesus, the Jew, will no longer divide Jews and Christians but unite them," according to David Flusser.[29]

The well-known Jewish philosopher Martin Buber calls Jesus "his brother," as does Schalom ben Chorin after him. To him Jesus is not God, nor, did he ever claim to be. Buber regards Christian doctrine in this respect a distortion for which especially Paul and John are responsible. The whole idea of the Incarnation seems to him to be in conflict with Old Testament belief in God. Nor is Jesus the Messiah, according to Buber. The Jew knows that our world, as it is today, is not a redeemed world. He discerns this unredeemed state of the world in his own skin, he can taste it with his tongue, and the burden of it rests heavily on him. What further evidence for the unredeemed state of the world is necessary besides the bleeding body of the Jewish people? he asks. Buber cites as the two foci of the Jewish psyche the two fundamental and secularized convictions of the Jews: the non-incarnation of the self-revealing God and the unbroken continuity of history. In these respects Judaism and Christianity are separated from each other by an unbridgeable gap.[30]

The fundamental mistake of Christians, according to Buber, is their attempt to tie God down to this revelation. "We do not say that God cannot reveal himself. But we do not attribute to any of his revelations that quality of non-surpassability, to any the character of incarnation. God transcends every one of his manifestations. For Christianity this hiddenness, this imagelessness of God, is not enough: they

29. Flusser, *Tussen oorsprong en schisma*, p. 269.

30. For a summary and discussion of Buber's ideas on this point, cf. E. Flesseman van Leer, "De afwijzing van het christendom door Martin Buber" in *Op het spoor van Israël; Studies over het gesprek met Israël* (The Hague: Boeken centrum N.V., 1961), p. 132.

have 'captured' him in the image of Jesus Christ; for Christians he now has acquired this face."[31]

The immediate relation between man and God has been disturbed by Jesus Christ, who blocks the possibility of direct access. The real man Jesus is not to blame for this, says Buber, but his image is the one which came to the Gentile nations, especially through the work of Paul and John. Still, in another place Buber admits—cf. Fr. Rosenzweig—that this image of Jesus, this figure of the mediator, was perhaps indispensable for the nations of the world. After all, they were not united to God in a fundamental way, as Israel was, by an eternal covenant. For that reason the Gentile nations would not have been able to enter into a relationship with this non-incarnate, ever-transcendent, always-retreating God without a mediator. Buber does not wish to render any judgment about the significance of Jesus for the nations of the world. But for Israel Jesus is not the incarnate Word, nor the conclusive and absolute revelation of God, nor the mediator.[32]

In Buber's writings, as in those of many other Jewish authors, the messianic *task* of the nation occupies a larger place than the *person* of the Messiah. He calls Judaism a religion of redemption, not a religion of a redeemer. Jesus' mistake, according to Buber, is that he is the first to break his incognito and so betrays the messianic secret. Buber goes to great lengths in his rejection of Jesus. As a Jew he not only rejects "the Christ of the church," but believes he also has to reject "the Jesus of early Jewish Christianity." By his auto-messianism, Jesus, though standing in and being the product of the tradition of Israel, has in Buber's opinion overstepped the boundary which God has set for man.[33]

Schalom ben Chorin, whose work proceeds further

31. Van Leer, pp. 133, 134.
32. Van Leer, pp. 135, 136.
33. Van Leer, pp. 143, 146.

along this line, describes the schism in these words: "The faith *of* Jesus unites us; faith *in* Jesus separates us."[34]

"For me," says ben Chorin, "Jesus is the eternal brother, not just my human brother but my Jewish brother. I discern the brotherly hand which grasps me that I may follow him. But it is not the hand of the messiah, the hands that have been marked by wounds. It is definitely not a divine but a human hand in whose lines the deepest suffering has been engraved."[35] According to ben Chorin, Jesus was no Messiah, God, or son of God, nor a prophet, but a very radical, critically independent, teacher who was spiritually akin to the Pharisees. He distinguishes three phases in Jesus' inner development: (a) the period in which he expected the imminent breakthrough of the kingdom of God (Matt. 10:23); (b) the period of interiorization (Luke 17:21: "the kingdom of God is within you" [NIV]); and (c) his self-sacrifice. His life ends on the cross with the cry: "My God, my God, why hast Thou forsaken me?" Though it failed tragically, in Jewish eyes this does not diminish Jesus' greatness. After all, Rabbi Akiba ben Joseph was also mistaken when in the second revolt against the Romans he held Bar Kochba to be the Messiah, only to die as a martyr himself. Despite this, he remains a very authoritative scriptural scholar.[36] Whether Christians are right in believing in the resurrection, says ben Chorin, is a question which lies outside our purview. At this point the history of Jesus ends and the history of Christ begins. The most important fact, in his opinion, is that again and again Jesus arose in the hearts of people who met him, like Paul on the way to Damascus.[37]

34. Ben Chorin, *Bruder Jesu*, p. 11.

35. Ben Chorin, *Bruder Jesu*, p. 12.

36. Schalom ben Chorin, *Jesus im Judentum* (Wuppertal: Brockhaus, 1970), p. 45.

37. Cf. the summary of M. de Jonge, *Jezus inspirator en spelbreker* (Nijkerk: Callenbach, 1971), pp. 119, 120.

It is not my intent here to offer an account of the
historical development of the Jewish understanding of Jesus
or of the split between church and synagogue. But I do want
to cite the view that from the time of the destruction of
Jerusalem by the Romans Christology developed along
lines which were to make impossible any further symbiosis
between Jewish Christians and the Jewish synagogue.[38]

Today, too, David Flusser asserts that it is Christology
which is responsible for the schism between Jews and
Christians. In his opinion, Christology blossomed especially in those New Testament passages which were originally written in Greek: the epistles, and much less so the
synoptic gospels. Christology exerted a strong attraction
among non-Jews who felt a sense of kinship with Judaism.
By means of this Christology, a faith which was Jewish in
origin, they were now able to compensate for their inferior
position with respect to "real" Jews. David Flusser calls
Jesus' teaching Jewish. In his opinion the same adjective
applies to Christology and all of its subdivisions. On the
one hand, Christology developed out of Jesus' strong sense
of self-esteem and his history; on the other, it came out of
the different fundamental motifs of the Jewish religion
which were associated with Jesus. He sees rabbinical and
hellenistic Judaism as the appropriate point of connection
for explaining the Jewish origins of the church's Christology. What happened was that Jesus' own experience of
sonship was linked with the Jewish conception of the
preexistence of the Messiah. This paved the way for the
idea that Jesus also possessed a divine nature (a hypostasis
of God): that the Son "reflects the glory of God and bears
the very stamp of his nature, upholding the universe by his

38. K. Hruby, "Die Trennung von Kirche und Judentum," in *Judentum und Kirche: Volk Gottes,* Theologische Berichte 3 (Cologne: Ben ziger
Verlag, 1974), pp. 152, 153.

word of power" and that through him God created the
world (Heb. 1:2, 3).

The Jewish view that the death of martyrs confers the
forgiveness of sins was transferred, as something self-
evident, to Jesus' death by crucifixion. Even the experience
of his resurrection is Jewish, as well as the notion of his
ascension to heaven. The whole of Christology is a sublime
expression of the tendency, prevalent at the time of the
second temple, to re-mythologize Judaism. According to
Flusser, Christology demonstrates to the limit the possibilities of this process of re-mythologizing.

In the early post-apostolic period, Christianity draws
out the implications of this Christology. People not only
believe that Christ is divine but even refer to him as God.
This already occurs in the thought of Ignatius of Antioch (ca.
70-107). Later the doctrine of the holy Trinity is developed
primarily to stave off bitheism. Considering the basis of the
Jewish stress on monotheism it is hard to see how Judaism
would ever have been able to adopt full belief in the divinity
of Christ. This difference between Judaism and the Christianity of the church fathers is reflected in the writings of the
rabbis. There, as in Islam, the idea that God has a son, and
that this son is divine, is repudiated.

For the majority of Jews, says Flusser, even the Christology of the New Testament was already unacceptable. He
sees a fundamental distinction between the gospels and
Acts on the one hand, and the remaining New Testament
writings on the other. Information about the historical Jesus
in the New Testament, apart from the gospels and Acts, is
decidedly fragmentary. What we do find is a large-scale
unfolding of the christological drama, one that begins with
creation and extends, by way of the Jesus of Nazareth, to the
end of time: *that* is the real content of Christianity. The faith
of Jesus is one we know solely from the gospels; faith *in*
Christ is primarily developed outside the synoptic gospels.

The primary Hebrew stratum of the synoptic gospels, according to Flusser, does not reflect the Christology of the church. Also the Christology of all known Jewish-Christian groups is defective.

Of course it is impossible to know, concludes Flusser, how far this Christology had crystallized and settled before it became the cornerstone of non-Jewish Christianity. Christology in this form, however, and not the faith of Jesus, is the main content of the Christian religion. When Christianity becomes mainly the faith of Gentiles the centrifugal force of the Christological system becomes considerably more effective in its anti-Jewish consequences.[39]

It is not my intent, nor is this the place, to enter into dialogue with Flusser and other quoted authors concerning the issue of how Jesus' image can be reconstructed from the gospels and epistles (cf. the final chapter). It was my intention to let Jewish scholars speak for themselves. In the introduction to his book *Jesus the Jew*, Geza Vermes remarks: "If, after working his way through the book, the reader recognizes that this man, so distorted by Christian and Jewish myth alike, was *in fact* neither the Christ of the church, nor the apostate and bogeyman of Jewish popular tradition, some small beginning may have been made in the repayment to him of a debt long overdue."[40] Who was he then? "Jesus the just man, the *zaddik*, Jesus the helper and healer, Jesus the teacher and leader, venerated by his intimates and less committed admirers alike as prophet, lord, and *son of God*."[41]

One wonders: when it comes to understanding the importance of Jesus Christ, will the schism between church and synagogue ever be undone?

---

39. Flusser, *Tussen oorsprong en schisma*, pp. 307, 310, 311, 313, 314, 315.

40. G. Vermes, *Jesus the Jew* (London: Collins, 1973), p. 17.

41. Vermes, p. 225.

In his well-known study of Paul, Hans Joachim Schoeps declares:

> Thus difference as well as affinity becomes clear: the Messianism of Israel is directed towards that which is to come, while the eschatology of the universal Christian church looks for a return of Him who has come. Both are united in the common expectation that the decisive event is still to come, that event which will disclose the consummation of God's ways with men, already partially and differently manifested in His dealings with Israel and the church. The church of Jesus Christ has kept no picture of its Savior and Lord. But it might well be that He who comes at the end of time, He who has been alike the expectation of the synagogue and the church, will bear one and the same countenance.[42]

Pinchas Lapide says something similar when he remarks: "I am happily prepared to wait until the coming one comes, and if he should show himself to be Jesus of Nazareth, I cannot imagine that even a single Jew who believes in God would have the least thing against that. . . . If he would only come!"[43]

"It seems to me," writes David Flusser, "that very few Jews would protest if the messiah, when he comes, should turn out to be the Jew Jesus."[44]

42. H. J. Schoeps, *Paul—The Theology of the Apostle in the Light of Jewish Religious History* (Philadelphia: Westminster, 1961), p. 258.

43. P. Lapide and Jürgen Moltmann, *Jewish Monotheism and Christian Trinitarian Doctrine* (Philadelphia: Fortress, 1981), p. 79.

44. D. Flusser, "Jezus als vraag aan joden en christenen" *Concilium* XI, 8 (1974): 133.

II THE CHRIST OF THE MUSLIMS

The Messiah, Jesus, son of Mary, was only the Messenger of God, and his Word . . . and a Spirit. . . .

The Koran, 4:168

IN this chapter we shall be confronted by the Christ of the Muslims. First, we shall see how the holy book of the Muslims, the Koran, speaks of Jesus; next, we shall stop to consider an image of Jesus as Muslims today picture him, being assisted especially by the work of the Egyptian novelist Naguib Maḥfūẓ.

Jesus occupies a special place in the Koran and in Islam. A response to the figure of Jesus has been prevalent in the history of Islam, beginning with the prophet Muhammed himself. The image of Jesus offered in the Koran plays a decisive role in all of later Islamic history, although the mystical tradition in Islam developed its own Jesus-image, one differing, but not entirely detached, from both that of the Koran and the New Testament.

From the perspective of the New Testament, no doubt, the information which the Koran offers concerning Jesus is very sparse and fragmentary, comparable to the image of Jesus found in the twelfth chapter of Revelation. There one reads of a woman bearing a child who is subsequently caught up into heaven. In this account the life of Jesus between his birth and his ascension has, as it were, dropped out. Similarly, in the Koran Jesus' birth is reported twice but only a very small part of his public ministry is recounted.

JESUS IN THE KORAN

The face of Jesus which shines from the pages of the Koran is "high honored . . . in this world and the next, near stationed to God" (3:45 [40]).* God made him "Blessed" (19:31 [32]).

The Koran was revealed to Muhammed over a period of twenty-two or twenty-three years. The first part came to the prophet in Mecca from ca. A.D. 610 to 622, the year of the *hegira*, the flight from Mecca to Medina. In Medina, until Muhammed's death in 632, the second part was "sent down" to him. From these two periods, the Meccan and the Medinese, some ninety-five verses dealing with Jesus have come down to us. In the Koran Jesus is usually introduced as "Jesus the son of Mary."

Compared with Jesus' portrait in the four gospels, the one given in these verses is extremely fragmentary. It is fairly well established that Muhammed himself never read the New Testament. It must be granted, however, that what the Koran says about Jesus is to a degree consistent with, or at least reminiscent of, the New Testament. In some instances the Koran offers parallels to what the church calls the apocryphal gospels. Some facts have been put in a Koranic framework and have thus acquired a special color. Then again, the Koran contains facets of the image of Jesus

* The quotations are from A. J. Arberry, *The Koran Interpreted*, 2 vols. (New York: Macmillan, 1955). Where two verse references are given, the bracketed one refers to this "translation."

in which it seems the mysteries of the Christian faith have
been neglected or denied.

The birth of Jesus is announced to Mary by angels (or
a messenger of God, 19:19): "Mary, God has chosen thee,
and purified thee; He has chosen thee above all women"
(3:42 [37]).

Twice the Koran tells the story of the birth of Jesus, a
subject on which the New Testament has essentially very
little to say, except for the accounts in Luke 2 and Matthew
1. In the Koran account (19:22-27), Mary's relatives express
consternation over the impropriety of the event; Mary
responds by pointing to the child in the cradle. In aston-
ishment her relatives wonder how they are going to speak
to a child in a cradle. And then a miracle: the child speaks
like an adult (cf. 3:46 [41]; 5:110), giving proof of a perfect
awareness of his mission, which sounds "Islamic." He
says: "Lo, I am God's servant; God has given me the Book,
and made me a Prophet. Blessed He has made me,
wherever I may be; and He has enjoined me to pray *(salāt)*
and to give the alms *(zakāt)*, so long as I live" (19:30, 31; cf.
the passage from vs. 27 on). *Salāt*, ritual prayer, and *zakāt*,
giving alms, in time became two of the five pillars of Islam
(in addition to profession of faith, fasting, and the pilgrimage to Mecca).

The Koran emphasizes that Jesus could perform
miracles. He made birds of clay and breathed life into them
(3:49 [43]; cf. 5:110), a familiar story from the apocryphal
Gospel of Thomas, the so-called "infancy"gospel. Jesus
heals the blind and leprous and raises the dead (3:49 [43];
5:110). Later in his ministry there is mention of a table which
he caused to descend from heaven (5:114), one of the last
references to Jesus in the Koran. This miracle reminds one
of the table which Peter, in his vision, saw coming down
from heaven (Acts 10). The word for "table" the Koran uses
here is of Ethiopian origin and means "table of the Lord."

Jesus not only performed miracles—he himself was a miracle, a sign (*āya*) from God. Though he encounters unbelief, the apostles are on his side and say, "We will be helpers of God; we believe in God; witness thou our submission" ("witness that we are Muslims" in Arabic!) (3:52 [45]). "And a party of the children of Israel believed, and a party disbelieved" (61:14). "And the unbelievers among them said, 'This is nothing but sorcery manifest'" (5:110).

Jesus regards himself the Messenger of God (61:6), and is called his Word and Spirit (4:169). It is said of him that he was confirmed with the Holy Spirit (2:81; 2:253; 5:110 [109]). He identifies himself as a prophet (19:30 [31]). Next to Noah, Abraham, and Moses he is among the prophets with whom God has made a covenant (33:7). He is also called Messiah (3:40; 4:156), though the title does not appear to have the original biblical content here. He is said to be no more than a servant of God (4:170; 43:59). He was nothing other than a messenger who, like Mary his mother, ate food (5:79). Along with Noah, Abraham, and Moses, he is one of the greatest of the prophets (cf. 30:7; 2:254).

The birth of Jesus is compared with that of Adam regarding the manner in which God created him: "Truly, the likeness of Jesus, in God's sight, is as Adam's likeness; He created him of dust, then said He unto him, 'Be,' and he was" (3:59 [52]). It was Jesus who brought the Gospel. God taught him the Book, the Wisdom, the Torah, and the Gospel (3:43). He is pictured as the one who confirmed that which had come before him, the Torah. The Gospel, like the Torah, contains "guidance and light" (5:50; cf. 57:26).

In a context that refers to Jews, the Koran says they do not believe in Jesus (3:45; 61:6, 14); further, they plotted against him (3:54 [47]) and spread slander about Mary (4:156 [155]). Then follows a text usually construed as a denial of the crucifixion of Jesus. It reads: "And for their (the Jews') saying: 'We slew the Messiah, Jesus son of Mary, the Messenger of God'—yet they did not slay him, neither crucified him, only a likeness of that was shown to them" (4:156).

The Koran charges Christians with having accepted Jesus the Messiah as lord (9:31). Christians say that the Messiah is the Son of God (9:30). But the Koran regards as unbelievers those who say that God is the Messiah, Mary's son (5:19). Christians are wrong when they say that he is the Son of God and that he and his mother are gods (5:116), for God can destroy them both (5:17 [19]).

The Koran warns Christians not to speak of "Three" with regard to God (4:171 [169]), nor to make Jesus one of the "Three" (5:73 [77]). Jesus himself is cited to refute such a notion (cf. 5:72 [76], 116 [116]). Jesus is also said to have predicted the coming of the prophet Muhammed ("who shall come after me, whose name shall be Ahmad"—61:6), and to have knowledge of the (last) hour (34).

Of Jesus it is said that God raised him up to himself (4:158 [156]; cf. 3:55 [48]). On Resurrection Day Jesus will be a witness against those who do not believe in him (4:159 [157]).

This brief survey of Koranic texts concerning Jesus is enough to bring out the fragmentariness of the image of Jesus in the Koran and to raise the question whether the Christian mysteries are repudiated by the Koran. Is the deity of Jesus actually denied ("The Messiah is not God"; "He is not one of the Three") and the crucifixion as well? These are oft-repeated questions.

In all these cases, does the Koran reject Christian orthodoxy itself or only certain Christian dogmatic and possibly heretical notions? At the very least it is striking that in some respects the Koran's criticism of Christian ideas coincides with Jewish objections. Jews, too, opposed the identification of Jesus with God, the practice of calling him "son of God" and speaking of the "Trinity."

There are reasons for suggesting that what the Koran

rejects are not authentic Christian notions. There is, for example, the fact that, in rejecting this idea of Jesus as "son of God" one rejects the idea of "carnal" descent. God simply cannot have children—neither son nor daughter—because he could not have taken a wife (6:101; 72:2 [3]). From the earliest beginning of Muhammed's public actions in Mecca such a polytheistic idea was rejected: "He (God) has not begotten, and has not been begotten" (112:3).

Statements like "God has taken to Him a son" (2:110; 19:36, etc.) indicate that the deity of Jesus was understood more as the deification of a human being than as the incarnation of God. The Trinity was obviously regarded more as a triad, perhaps even as consisting of God, Jesus, and Mary (5:116). The crucifixion of Jesus is denied in one passage, while his death is clearly told in others (19:34). As far as the cross and what it means for redemption, one can say perhaps that these matters are not so much denied as ignored by the Koran.[1]

A MODERN ISLAMIC IMAGE OF JESUS

The Koranic image of Jesus has continued to be authoritative for and to exert influence over all later discourse on Jesus by Muslims, right up to the present time. Very often such discourse has been polemical and directed against Christians. But there are also other voices, voices that we should hear, without any claim made that they are repre-

1. I have enlarged upon this subject further in my *De moslimse naaste* (Kampen: Kok, 1978). See the literature cited there. Further, my "De Christus van de Moslims" in *Rondom het Woord* 20 (Sept. 1978): 33-38, and *De Nieuwe arabische mens* (Baarn: Ten Have, 1977), pp. 54-66; C. Schedl, *Muhammed und Jesus; die christologisch relevante Texte des Korans* (Vienna: Herder, 1978); T. Baarda, "Jezus in de mystiek van de Islam," in *Gereformeerd Theologisch Tijdschrift* 78 (Aug. 1978): 175-86.

sentative for Islam and Muslims in general. They offer a point of departure for a real dialogue between Christians and Muslims about the significance of Jesus Christ. The Algerian scholar 'Ali Merad has written an impressive account of the figure of Jesus in the Koran. He warns his fellow Muslims that they must not think they possess the complete truth about Jesus. True, some things in the Koran are asserted with certainty, but other statements are intended for further joint reflection with Christians. He also thinks that much modern Christian scholarship on the New Testament offers perspectives for such common reflection.[2]

I shall confine myself here to reproducing an entirely unique and very special image of Jesus, namely, that which has been depicted by the well-known Egyptian novelist Naguib Maḥfūẓ, who won the Nobel prize for literature in 1988.

Some years ago—it was 1959 and done in serial form (a form of pre-publication frequently used in the Arab world)—Naguib Maḥfūẓ wrote a book entitled *The Children of our Quarter,* a five-part novel. The author's intent in this work was to describe the history of the fortunes and (especially) misfortunes of humankind. In these five connected stories he narrates the history of people and that of the "prophets" as though it had all taken place in Cairo— appropriately so since Cairo is known as "the mother of the world." He relates how, whenever someone is sad and complains of an injustice or ill-treatment, he or she points to the big house at one end of the quarter and says sadly:

> "This is the house of our ancestor. We are all his descendants and are entitled to his estate. Why should we be hungry and ill-treated?"
> Then he relates one of the stories, citing the life histories

2. A. Merad, "Language Commun et dialogue," *Islamochristiana* I (1975): 6.

of Adham, Jabal, Rifāʾa, and Qāsim, famous children of our neighborhood and our ancestor.

"This grandfather is a great mystery. . . . A long time ago he withdrew into his big house. And ever since that time no one has seen him anymore. The story of his withdrawal and his age is very perplexing. It may be that the stories have been spun out of someone's imagination and desires. A fact is that he is called al-Jabalāwī, and in consequence our quarter bears the same name. He is the owner of everything in sight. . . . One time I heard someone speak about him and say: 'He is the source of our quarter and our quarter is the source of Egypt, the mother of the world. . . .' Someone else remarked: 'In reality he was a bully *(futuwa)*, but his conduct in the country was not proud and he was merciful toward the weak.' "[3]

"How often," continues the narrator, "am I not moved to go to the big house to try to get a glimpse of him, but it is in vain. The windows are closed and betray the absence of life. Is it not distressing that we have such an ancestor—one we do not see and who does not see us? Is it not strange that he remains hidden behind the locked doors of the big house and that we have to live in the dirt? And when I ask what has happened to him and why we have to live as we do, then I immediately get to hear these stories and I repeat to you the names of Adham, Jabal, Rifāʾa, and Qāsim."[4]

The successive stories which Naguib Maḥfūẓ relates are in fact "transpositions" of stories about Adam (Adham), Moses (Jabal), Jesus (Rifāʾa), and Mohammed (Qāsim). The fifth and final story is about ʾArafa, a name which stands for modern man, the man of knowledge and science, the man of today.[5]

3. Naguib Maḥfūẓ, *Awlād Haritna* (Beirut: Dar al-Adab, 1967), pp. 5, 6.

4. Maḥfūẓ, p. 6.

5. Cf. my article "Naguib Maḥfūẓ and Secular Man," in *Humaniora Islamica* (The Hague: Mouton, 1974), pp. 105-19, and *A Modern Arabic Biography of Muhammed* (Leiden: Brill, 1972), pp. 24-29.

Naguib Maḥfūẓ uses material both from the Bible and the Koran, but he makes everything happen in the context of Cairo, in a quarter of the city in which he himself was born, in the fashion of children who picture the biblical or other stories as happening in their own surroundings.

The name Adham easily suggests that of Adam. Jabal, a word literally meaning "mountain," is perhaps intentionally "related" to the name al-Jabalāwī, the name for God. It suggests the close "kinship" among Moses, the Jewish people, and God. The name Rifāʿa can be translated as "the Exalted One." In the Koran it is said of Jesus that "God will raise him to himself" (3:48) and "God raised him up" (4:156). Qāsim is the name for Muhammed, possibly inspired by the fact that Muhammed had a son named Qāsim.

Each time we are told how each of these figures tried to maintain or restore justice and righteousness in the quarter so that it is ruled in a way intended by al-Jabalāwī. But over and over tyranny returns and grows: it is the rule of those who in lawless ways have taken control over "the goods of this world," goods intended for all. All are descendants of al-Jabalāwī ("children of one Father") and have equal rights to a share in the goods.

The plain object of these stories is to show how the three great religions—Judaism, Christianity, and Islam—have sought, through their "prophets"—Moses, Jesus, and Muhammed—to bring about social justice.

In the concluding story Naguib Maḥfūẓ writes about ʾArafa, a man who no longer believes in those "stories" about Adham, Rifāʿa, and Qāsim, and who by his own power and knowledge tries to achieve that justice for all.

Our concern here is with the author's portrayal of the figure of Rifāʿa or Jesus.

Whereas Moses (Jabal), according to the account of Naguib Maḥfūẓ, tries to bring about social justice within the structure of society, and Muhammed (Qāsim) tries to establish justice with the aid of violence, Jesus (Rifāʾa) concentrates on spiritual change.

In his allegorical narratives Naguib Maḥfūẓ exploits not only material from the Koran but also some from the Bible, in the process offering an image of Jesus that differs from the classic one usually presented in Islamic circles. Thus, for Naguib Maḥfūẓ Jesus was undoubtedly killed. The following dialogue occurs between Sādiq, a friend of Qāsim (Muhammed [perhaps Abū Bakr is meant]), and Zakariyya, his uncle (Abū Talib). Sādiq emphatically states: "Don't forget that al-Jabalāwī has chosen him (Qāsim = Muhammed) over all the other strong boys and I don't think that he (al-Jabalāwī = God) will abandon him in time of misfortune." Offended, Zakariyya replies: "This was also said in the days of Rifāʾa (Jesus), but he was killed nevertheless, right by the house of al-Jabalāwī."[6]

Repeatedly in these stories Jesus and Muhammed are compared—always a delicate point in the dialogue or polemic between Christians and Muslims.[7] In the story concerning Qāsim (Muhammed), this question is raised: "How can a man live without possessions?" The old man Yaḥyā answers: "By living like Rifāʾa. Qāsim, however, says that with possessions and the destruction of the strong boys the quarter will attain the dignity to which Jabal led his quarter and the love to which Rifāʾa called people and the happiness of which Adham dreamed."[8]

The story of Rifāʾa in Maḥfūẓ's novel deserves to be reproduced at greater length because it shows how this important Egyptian author pictured Jesus.

As was said earlier, the name Rifāʾa is rooted perhaps in the idea that Jesus was "raised" *(rafaʾa)* by God to himself.

6. Maḥfūẓ, p. 357.
7. Cf. my *De moslimse naaste,* esp. chap. 4.
8. Maḥfūẓ, p. 364.

In the Koran the word occurs twenty-nine times, but in the sense of "being raised by God" it is used only with reference to Jesus: "I will raise thee to Me" (3:48), and "God raised him up to Him" (4:156).[9]

> Amm Shāfī, a middle-aged carpenter, and 'Abda (Mary), while in exile outside Jabal's quarter (the Jewish quarter) have a child in Suq Mukattam (Mukattam is a mountain near Cairo). 'Abda (Mary) says to Amm Shāfī (Joseph): "O, if only you had been patient, Shāfī! Have you not heard people tell that our ancestor al-Jabalāwī is certain at some time to return from his isolation to save his children from injustice and humiliation?" (215).

Later, after the death of Zonfol (Herod), Shāfī, 'Abda, and Rifā'a return to their own quarter.

> Rifā'a, tall, slightly built, open-faced, is an attractive young man, with an air of gentleness and friendliness. He seems a stranger on the earth. When he looks at the big house and asks if it is the house of the ancestor, 'Abda answers: "Yes— you know we told you about it; your ancestor lives there, the owner of all this land and everything on it. . . . If he had not withdrawn from it the whole quarter would be filled with light" (218).
> A blind story-teller who felt Rifā'a's face exclaimed: "Astonishing! How like your grandfather you are!" (219).

It soon becomes evident that it is not Rifā'a's ambition to remain in his father's carpentry shop. He loves to listen to stories like those about Jabal and wants to know the secrets of the evil spirits so he can exorcize them.[10]

---

9. H. Michaud, *Jésus selon le Coran* (Neufchatel: Éditions Delachaux et Niestlé, 1960), p. 72.

10. Michaud, pp. 229ff.; cf. G. Vermes, in *Jesus the Jew* (London: Collins, 1973), who speaks emphatically about Jesus as exorcist.

When Umm B'khatirha asks him why he wants to know the secrets of exorcism he answers with conviction: "The wisdom of your work is that you overcome evil with the good and the beautiful" (234).

When an opportunity arises for him to enter marriage to a daughter of one of the "rulers," Rifāʿa rejects it:

"How can I be the son-in-law of the devil when my whole concern is to drive out the devil?" (236).

When in a certain context someone says:

"Violence—without it there can be no justice," Rifāʿa emphatically replies: "Fact is, our quarter needs mercy" (245).

Rifāʿa tells the story of how one day, while resting beneath the wall of the big house, he heard a voice as though it were speaking to itself in the dark. "Suddenly I was overwhelmed by the feeling that it was the voice of our grandfather Jabalāwī." "What gives you the idea that it was Jabalāwī's voice?" Shāfī asks. To which Rifāʿa vehemently replies: "It is not an idea, father. I shall give you proof. As soon as I heard the voice, I got up and turned to the house, going backward in order to be able to see it better. But I only saw darkness. . . . I heard the voice say that Jabal (Moses) had fulfilled his task and had given satisfaction but that the times had gotten worse than before. . . . I shouted: "Grandfather, Jabal is dead and others have taken his place. Stretch out your hand and help us." "I hope by God that no one heard you," said Shāfī (247, 248).

Rifāʿa's eyes shone: "My grandfather heard me." Again the voice sounded: "How wrong it is for a young man to ask his old grandfather to act: the beloved son is the one to act." I ask: "What means can I who am weak employ against the leaders?" and he answered: "The real weakling is the fool who does not know his own inner strength, and I do not like fools. . . ." Rifāʿa said, his face shining, "and now I know what is expected of me. . . ." "Does anyone ask anything of

you? comes back Shāfī. "Yes! I am weak but I am not a fool.
The beloved son is the one who acts." Shāfī warns him that
he will be destroyed, to which, smiling, Rifāʿa replies: "They
only kill those who have permitted their eyes to focus on
possessions (the good of the world). . . ." "And have you let
your eyes fall on something other than the goods of the
world?" asks Shāfī. Full of confidence came back the voice
of Rifāʿa: "Adham longed for a life of pure happiness; Jabal
also, and he saw the goods only as a way leading to such a
life; but he had the idea that it was not attainable for a person
unless the estate were equally divided and everyone received his share and enjoyed the usufruct of the property.
But the estate is such a small matter; it can be had without
really living. Everyone who wants it can have it. . . . It is
within our power to be rich from this moment on. . . . The
estate means nothing, father: the happiness of a contented
life is everything. Only the hidden demons deep within us
stand between us and our happiness. It is not for nothing
that I like the knowledge of evil spirits and am perfecting it.
Perhaps it is the will of the Lord of heaven which has
brought me to this" (248, 249).

Rifāʿa began to visit the poor and to cast out evil spirits
(250). At a given time he marries a woman in order to save
her, although the marriage is not consummated. Later she
will betray him.

One time when he left his house a woman who did not
belong to the Jabalites (Jews) approached him and cordially
said to him: "Good morning, master Rifāʿa!" He was struck
by the tone of respect in which she spoke and the manner in
which she pronounced his name and title. He asked her:
"What do you want?" She said, imploring him: "I hope you
can heal him." Like all Jabalites, he looked down on other
people of the quarter and, lest his own people would despise
him even more, he did not want to help her. He asked: "Is
there no exorcist in the quarter?" In tears she answered: "Yes,
but I am a poor woman." Then Rifāʿa relented, and he
rejoiced that she should seek his help (265).

In conversation with Yasmīna (his wife), Rifāʿa asked
why she told people she was a Jabalite:

> "So that they will know that I am superior to them all." Then
> he said: "You will be better off and feel better, too, if you
> overcome your vanity. The Jabalites are not the best people
> in our quarter. The best people are those who do the most
> good. I used to make the same mistake. . . . But the people
> who deserve happiness are those who sincerely seek it. Look
> at the way the poor accept me and are healed of evil spir-
> its. . . . You are a Jabalite and all of the Jabalites, even my own
> father, refuse to submit to my healing power. . . ." In the new
> quarter, he was called Master Rifāʿa, in a sincere and loving
> way. He was known as the man who delivered people from
> evil spirits and gave them happiness and health, all for the
> sake of God alone (266, 267).

*   *   *

It is clear throughout that Naguib Maḥfūẓ views
Rifāʿa's work as "spiritual," not political, although he is
aware that Rifāʿa is still feared by those in power and regarded as a threat, a reason why the rulers want to liquidate
him! In conversation with ʾAlī, Rifāʿa says,

> "How people have suffered for the sake of their wretched
> possessions and blind power. Cursed be the possession of
> goods and power." Rifāʿa cries out: "All that time . . . when
> Jabalāwī asked Jabal to make the houses of his quarter like
> the big house in splendor and beauty, people desired the
> power and splendor of Jabalāwī himself. They have forgot-
> ten his other attributes. That is the reason why Jabal could
> not change people simply by gaining rights to the estate for
> them. For that reason, the moment he died, the strong boys
> took over the estate again and the weak were filled with hate.
> Misery returned. But I open the gates of happiness without
> any estate or power" (268, 269).

Someone says: "They (the Jabalites) spread strange sto-

ries about the estate and the ten conditions as though
Jabalāwī were only *their* ancestor."

It turns out that Rifāʿa's public role, though nonpoliti-
cal, is still bringing him into confrontation with the authorities. What the chief administrator most feared was that
people would feel there was power in solidarity which
enabled them to rise up against the leaders. For that reason
he deemed it necessary to destroy Rifāʿa. But to avoid a
general conflict he needed the consent of Khonfis, the leader
of the Jabalites (270-82).

In Khonfis's presence a certain man named Bayūmī subjected Rifāʿa to an interrogation in the following manner:

"Why did you leave your quarter and your people?" He
simply replied: "No one answered my call." "Then what did
you want of them?" "Deliver them from the evil spirits
which spoiled their happiness." Bayūmī angrily asked: "Do
you suppose you are responsible for the happiness of
people?" "Yes—so long as I am able to realize it for them."
Bayūmī frowned: "People have heard you say that you
despise possessions and power." "It was to show them that
happiness does not lie in their imagination but in what I do."

Khonfis got angry and asked: "Does not that mean that
you despise people who have power and importance?"
Rather serenely he answered: "No sir, but it does mean that
happiness is not the same as power and importance."

With a penetrating look Bayūmī asked him: "People have
also heard you say that this is what the owner of the goods
(Jabalāwī) wants for them." His bright eyes became uneasy.
"Is that what they say?" "And what do you say?" For the
first time he hesitated. "I can only speak in accordance with
my own understanding. . . ." Bayūmī's eyes narrowed.
"They say that you repeat for them what you hear from
Jabalāwī himself." "That is how I understand his words to
Adham and Jabal."

Khonfis shouted: "His words to Jabal do not allow for
interpretation," and Bayūmī added: "You say that you have

heard Jabalāwī, and you say that this is what Jabalāwī wants; but no one can speak in the name of Jabalāwī save the overseer of his possessions and his heir. When Jabalāwī wants to say anything he will say it to him. He is responsible for his possessions and the executor of the ten conditions. You idiot—how can you despise power, importance, and riches in the name of Jabalāwī who is the owner of these things himself?"

To the end Rifāʾa heaved a sigh: "Why do people hate me when I have never hated anybody?" (279-82).

It is important to note that in the inevitable confrontation with the people in power Rifāʾa absolutely rejects the use of violence:

"Do not even think of fighting. One who tries to bring people happiness cannot lightly think of shedding their blood." (283).

Sadly Rifāʾa reflects on his thorny situation. He has loved others with all his heart and he has sought their happiness with so much devotion—how is it that he should now have to endure their hatred? And would Jabalāwī accept failure? Said Rifāʾa: "The need for healing is greatest where the sickness is worse" (285, 288).

In the night before the betrayal and downfall he had a meal with his friends and the wife who betrays him. The bread was broken and distributed and their hands met over their plates. It seemed as if they had become totally unaware of the death which hovered over their heads. Said Rifāʾa:

"Do not forget that it is our goal to heal, not to kill. It is better for a person to *be* killed than to kill." Yasmīna (his wife) said to Rifāʾa: "I am simply astonished that you are able to speak so cheerfully, as though you were at a wedding." Answered Rifāʾa: "You will get used to joy when as of tomorrow you will be free from the devil." Then, looking at his brothers, he remarked: "Some of you are ashamed to be peaceful, and we are children of a quarter which only respects the ways of the leaders, but true power does not lie in making threats. To

fight against evil spirits is much more difficult than to attack
the weak or to oppose the leaders" (289-90).

After Rifāʾaʾs arrest he was led toward the desert.

His eyes rested for a moment on the big house. Does the
ancestor know of his situation? Just one word from him
would be enough to save Rifāʾa from the clutches of these
tyrants and to ruin their plans. . . . Jabal was similarly driven
into a corner and he escaped and overcame his enemies. . . .
But he, Rifāʾa, did not hear a word from behind the wall. . . .
He felt lost, remembering that a woman had betrayed him
and that his friends had fled. . . . "Why do you want to kill
me?" he asked. Bayūmī cudgels him on the head and shouts
furiously at him. . . . Then, out of the depths of misery, Rifāʾa
cried out: " Jabalāwī! " (294, 295).

Later his friends, searching for him, found his body. One
of them, whose name is Kerim, sobbingly whispered: "Your
life was a short dream but it fills our hearts with love and
purity. We could not imagine that you would leave us so
soon, let alone that someone should kill you, some person
from our ungrateful quarter which you loved and served
and which only wanted to destroy the love, the mercy, and
healing you brought it." Another friend sighed: "Were it not
for your love which remains in us we would forever hate
people." And a third: "We shall have no peace of mind till
we have made up for our cowardice" (297, 298).

The separation from Rifāʾa was worse for them than death
and his absence was torture. Their only hope in life was to
honor his memory by reviving his mission and punishing
his murderers, as ʾAlī decided to do. . . . When the people of
his quarter, Shāfī and his closest friends, went out in search
of the body they did not find it. Neither did the leaders who
also looked for it (298, 299).

It seemed every trace of Rifāʾaʾs existence was gone but
some things remained which reminded them of him, like
Rifāʾaʾs house called the "House of Healing" and the faithful
friends who stayed in touch with his followers and taught
them the secret method of casting out evil spirits and healing

the sick. They were convinced that in this way they were bringing Rifā'a back to life. But 'Alī could find no peace until he cursed the evildoers. Husayn accused him to his face: "You are not Rifā'a's follower at all," but 'Alī shouted: "He was a leader, the greatest of all leaders, but his generosity deceived him" (302-3).

Finally, it is related that the Riphaites formed a separate section of the neighborhood, having the same rights and duties as the Jabal-quarter. 'Alī was made the overseer of their part of the estate.

In his death Rifā'a received more honor, respect, and love than when he lived. His life became a glorious story told over and over by everyone and sung about to the music of the *rabāba* (Arab musical instrument), especially the part about Jabalāwī who took his body and buried it in his garden. On this point there was agreement among the Riphaites (Christians) . . . but they differed about everything else.

Kerim, Husayn, and Zāki maintained that it had been Rifā'a's mission to heal the sick and that he despised status and power. . . . Some of his followers even avoided marriage in their eagerness to follow him. One of them called for the renewal of Rifā'a's quarter. It was claimed that Rifā'a did not despise worldly goods as such, but only wanted to demonstrate that real happiness can be found without them and that the evil spirits, which are evoked by greed, are to be condemned. When the revenues are fairly divided and used for good ends, they are completely acceptable and good (304-5).

It would be fascinating to reproduce the whole story. But enough is adduced here to give an impression of Maḥfūẓ's image of Jesus. It represents an enormous step in the direction of a "Christian" understanding of Jesus in that the crucifixion and death of Jesus, usually denied by Muslims on the basis of the usual Koran interpretation, occupy an important place in this narrative. It contains numerous allusions to the story in the gospels which everyone who is acquainted with it will recognize. As a result, it is a unique Islamic interpretation of Jesus and his significance not only for Cairo (mother of the world), but for the entire world.

III THE SCOURGED CHRIST

*The signs of the suffering of Christ, the Lord, [come through]
in the faces which are marked by the suffering of an
oppressed people.*

Puebla

IN this chapter I shall briefly touch upon the manner in
which the "Spanish Christ" was transmitted to Latin
America, beginning with Christopher Columbus and Francisco Pizarro. In contrast, there is the image of "Christ the
Liberator" as various theologians of liberation have "designed" it in partial reaction to the "Spanish Christ"
(Leonardo Boff, Jon Sobrino, Everardo Ramirez Toro).

It is important to realize that the voyages of discovery
made by the Portuguese and Spaniards from the fifteenth
century on occurred at a time when the reconquest of the
Iberian peninsula had been completed. For centuries a
society flourished in Spain (which Muslims called al-
Andalus), a symbiosis[1] of Jews, Christians, and Muslims.

In 1492 the fall of Grenada marked the end of the

---

1. S. D. Goitein, *Jews and Arabs. Their Contacts Through the Ages* (New
York: Schocken Books, 1964), describes that "symbiotic" society of Jews,
Christians, and Muslims.

reconquest of Spain from the Moors. This event also marked
the end of Islamic hegemony over the Iberian peninsula. In
the period of reconquest, a period which lasted for centuries, not only Muslims but also Jews were driven out of the
territory. Some 150,000 Jews were, in fact, eliminated from
the "most Christian" Spain of Ferdinand and Isabella.[2]
Many of these Jews sought and found refuge in Islamic
North Africa and other parts of the Arab world in the East.
The well-known Jewish thinker Maimonides, originally
from Cordoba, died near Cairo, Egypt, in 1204.

CHRISTOPHER ("THE CHRIST-BEARER") COLUMBUS

It is not altogether accidental that in the year of the
completed "reconquista" (1492), the "discovery" of America by the Genovese Christopher Columbus took place.
What drove people like Columbus to undertake these and
later voyages is a combination of "gain and godliness,"[3] and
decidedly in that order. "The spiritual Don Quixote and the
materialistic Sancho Panza both embarked for the Indies."
But "the relatives and progeny of the latter . . . were in-
finitely more numerous than those of the former."[4]

One of the reasons why such an undertaking could
even be conceived was the recently acquired knowledge
that the earth is not flat but round and therefore circum-
navigable. Whatever other motives may have been present

2. G. Galeano, *De aderlating van een continent; Vier eeuwen eco-
nomische exploitatie van Latijns Amerika* (Amsterdam: Van Gennep, 1974),
p. 22.
3. C. R. Boxer, *The Dutch Seaborne Empire 1600–1800* (Pelican, 1973),
who speaks of "Gain and Godliness" with reference to Dutch colonialism
in a later period.
4. J. A. MacKay, *The Other Spanish Christ: A Study in the Spiritual
History of Spain and South America* (New York, 1932), p. 29.

(presumably also the ordinary love of adventure), the fundamental goal was to sail around the world of Islam. In that way people sought finally to surmount the barrier of the Islamic world against which they had fought on so many fronts for so many centuries.

The legend which throughout the Middle Ages played a role in this regard was that of the priest-king John, a Christian prince who was alleged to live somewhere "behind" the Islamic world. An alliance with him, it was thought, would enable Christians to take the Muslims between tongs, as it were, and thus still realize the original goal of the crusades.[5] In the case of Columbus it is said that he was very conscious of his prophetic Christian name, namely, that he was the "Christ-bearer."[6]

The question which naturally arises from the name is how well he carried out the task his name implied. Did he transmit the Christ of Scripture or did he betray him, and how was Christ received, discovered, perceived by the Indians? Columbus himself wrote: "I travel . . . in the name of the Holy Trinity from whom I hope for victory." He viewed his great discovery as the fulfillment of an Old Testament prediction: The ships of Tarshish bring their sons from far, their silver and gold with them, in honor of the name of the Lord (Isa. 60:9).

This enterprise, to his mind, was another kind of crusade, as is evident from the fact that it was his ambition to bring "from the newly-discovered lands the amount of money necessary to equip an army of 10,000 cavalry and 10,000 infantry" and so "to rescue Jerusalem from the Turks."[7]

5. A. Mulders, *Missie-geschiedenis* (Bussum: Paul Brand, 1957), pp. 151, 189, 190.

6. MacKay, p. 102.

7. MacKay, p. 24.

On October 2, 1492, Columbus landed on the island Guanahani, one of the islands of the Bahamas, to which he gave the name San Salvador. Existing names of people and places were disregarded.[8] Our concern here is to ask how the encounter between the "Salvador" or "Savior," and what would later be called Latin America was to develop.

After eight centuries of "reconquista," the Spaniards accompanying Columbus were guided by three principles:

1. "That it is pleasing to God to kill and rob unbelievers";
2. "That warriors and priests form the noblest social class";
3. "That work is debasing; and that the land belongs to the crown and the nobility who conquer it." The church sanctions this conquest and shares in the ownership of the land.

These ideas play a predominant role in the "colonization and Christianization of the new lands."[9]

Without a doubt, the conquests of Latin America were barbarian and gruesome. In 1542, a year after the conquest of Peru by Francisco Pizarro, Bartholomé de Las Casas wrote a letter to Spanish King Charles I (as Charles V of the Holy Roman Empire): "Daily in the land of New Castile, atrocities are committed at which Christian humanity shudders to look upon. Heaven's vengeance will fall upon those who bear the guilt. Our Lord Jesus Christ is hourly crucified in New Castile.... Young Indian women are torn from their poor families and forced to serve the Spaniards' lusts. Many a Spaniard keeps a harem. I must say, this would become the Crescent far better than the spotless Cross."[10] (We shall

8. Mulders, p. 191; Enrique Dussel, *The History and Theology of Liberation* (Maryknoll, NY: Orbis, 1976), p. 24.

9. MacKay, pp. 29, 30.

10. Quoted by Claus Bussmann, *Who Do You Say? Jesus Christ in Latin American Theology* (Maryknoll, NY: Orbis, 1985), p. 7. (The date given in this English translation of the German original is not 1552, as in the text of this book, but 1542.—TRANS.)

not stop to consider this passing shot at Islam in this justified exposé of Spanish atrocities; presumably, it is more revelatory of the image which the Spaniards had of the Moors than of the Moors themselves.)

Bartholomé de Las Casas, author of *Brevissima Relación de la destrución de las Indias occidentales* (1552), exposes the brutal exploitation of the unfortunate Indians and their premature deaths. He referred to Spaniards as oppressors who considered themselves Christians, but who, on account of their conduct toward the Indians, were in peril of losing their own salvation. Unless they ceased to humiliate, violate, and exploit the Indians, they would, he believed, undoubtedly be damned. For, said he, it is impossible for one who does not "do righteousness" to be saved. To him, the salvation of Christians was more at risk than that of the heathen! Indians were "the poor"—in the evangelical sense—rather than "pagans." In a letter to the emperor, Las Casas goes so far as to say that if the conversion of the Indians cannot take place without their death and destruction, it would be better for them never to become Christian. To Las Casas, Christ speaks from among the Indians. He writes, "In India, I have seen Jesus Christ, our God, scourged, devastated, not once but a million times."

Already from this first letter we learn the abiding characteristics of the history of Latin America: (1) the inseparability of missionary activity from conquest; and (2) the Europeans' feeling of superiority toward the Indians.

In other words, the history of the Indians in Latin America from 1492 on is to be characterized as a history of suffering—five centuries of the pillage of a continent (Galeano). They have been economically exploited, culturally destroyed and alienated, and raped in matters of religion.[11]

---

11. G. Gutiérrez, *The Power of the Poor in History* (Maryknoll, NY: Orbis, 1983), pp. 194ff. (on Las Casas); Bussmann, p. 9.

From Pope Alexander VI, the Catholic kings received a *Motu proprio* (a papal decree in the form of a letter), dated back to 4 May 1493 called *Inter cetera*, which, as Prien explains, must not be interpreted as a "donation." It rather constitutes a recognition in international law by the pope as the highest authority in Christendom of the conquest already in effect of regions in "West-India," with the attendant obligation of the vassal to engage in mission.[12]

METHOD OF "TRANSMISSION"

How conquest and Christianization went hand in hand and how this combination affected the preaching of Christ can perhaps be best illustrated with the example of Francisco Pizarro. He was a swineherd from Extra Madura who could neither read nor write, but who succeeded as conquistador in gaining control over Cuzco, the center of the Incan empire in Peru.[13] In him as in no other man the love of gain and the practice of godliness went together.

The conquest was undertaken from a base in Panama in January 1531. Francisco Pizarro was accompanied by a number of priests, among whom was the Dominican Vicente Valverde. Priests were taken along to effect the conversion of the "natives."[14]

We are told that for every military incursion and before possession was taken of a given region, a lengthy and rhetorical official announcement was read to the Indians without benefit of an interpreter(!), in the presence of a notary, in which the local population was urged to convert

12. H. J. Prien, *Die Geschichte des Christentums in Lateinamerika* (Göttingen: Van den hoeck & Ruprecht, 1978), p. 64.

13. A. Mulders, p. 252

14. K. Scott Latourette, *Three Centuries of Advance*, vol. 3 of *A History of the Expansion of Christianity* (London: Harper, 1947), p. 145.

to the holy Catholic faith. The procedure was for Spanish soldiers to read the so-called *requirimiento*—embracing the text of the Apostles' Creed (in Castilian!)—to an Indian tribe and to ask for their agreement. If they refused, a holy war was unleashed on them.[15] "If you do not or if you maliciously delay in so doing I certify that with God's help I will advance powerfully against you and make war on you wherever and however I am able, and will subject you to the yoke and obedience of the church and of the majesties and take your women and children to be slaves, and as such I will sell and dispose of them as their majesties may order, and I will take your possessions and do you all the harm and damage that I can."[16]

Something similar is told after Pizarro had taken prisoner Atahualpa, king of the Incas. He was asked to submit to the Spanish king and to accept the Catholic faith. The following story describes the event. The Dominican Valverde approached the Inca monarch Atahualpa "with the cross in his right hand and the Bible in his left." Having made the sign of the cross over the royal captive, he proceeded to deliver the following homily:

> "I am a priest of God and I teach divine things to the Christians. I have come likewise to teach them to you. God who is one in essence and a Trinity of persons, created heaven and earth and all that they contain. He formed of clay Adam the first man and from one of his ribs Eve from whom we all descend. Our first parents having disobeyed their Creator, we have been born in sin, and no one would obtain divine grace nor go to heaven if Jesus Christ, who is the Son of God, had not become incarnate in the womb of the Virgin Mary and if He had not redeemed us by dying on

15. J. Delumeau, *Einde van het Christendom* (Hilversum: Gooi en Sticht, 1978), pp. 58, 59; L. Hanke, *Colonisation et conscience chrétienne aux XVIe siècle* (Paris: Plon, 1957), pp. 29-39.

16. Galeano, p. 23.

a cross. Jesus Christ arose from the dead and ascended to
heaven leaving the apostle St. Peter as his vicar on earth,
having put the whole world under his jurisdiction. The
Popes, who are the successors of St. Peter, govern the human
race, and all nations, in whatever part they live and
whatever their religion, should obey them. A Pope has given
all these lands to the kings of Spain that they may pacify the
unbelievers and bring them within the pale of the Catholic
Church, outside of which no one can be saved. Governor
Pizarro has come on this mission. You should, therefore, Sir,
consider yourself tributary to the Emperor, abandon the
worship of the sun and all idolatries which would lead you
to hell and accept the true religion. If you do so God will
reward you and the Spaniards will protect you against your
enemies." The Inca replied that he would be vassal to no
king. He denied the Pope's right to distribute lands that were
not his. He refused to change his own sun-god for a God
who had been put to death by the creatures he made, and
wanted to know where Valverde had learned such doctrines.
When the Dominican handed him the Bible the Inca took it
and threw it wrathfully to the ground.[17]

The Inca leader was held captive nine and a half
months. In 1534 a gigantic ransom arrived in Sevilla, one
room full of gold and two of silver, which Francisco Pizarro had ordered the Inca monarch to pay.[18] But instead
of releasing him, as promised, the Spaniards broke their
word and condemned Atahualpa to be burned. "Valverde,
who was chiefly responsible for the sentence, now approached the condemned man promising him that if he
became a Christian," the sentence would be commuted to
death by strangulation. "The Inca consented and was baptized, being given the name of John in honor of the Evan-

17. MacKay, pp. 34-36; W. H. Prescott, *The Conquest of Peru* (reprint,
New York: Dolphin Books, Doubleday & Co., 1847), pp. 244, 245. The
address was interpreted by a certain Felipillo.
    18. Galeano, p. 25.

gelist whose day it was. After baptism he was strangled on the terrible garrotte while the Spaniards stood around and chanted the creed."[19]

Protest against such conduct was not lacking even at that time, though it appears not to have been very effective.

In 1511, Antonio de Montesinō censured the conduct of the Spanish conquistadores from the pulpit, citing the words of Isaiah and John the Baptist. The burden of criticism was directed against forced labor *(encomienda)* and the enslavement of the Indians. According to Bartholomé de Las Casas, who as a boy in Seville watched the Indians whom Columbus after his first voyage had brought to Spain in 1493,[20] and who had written about the annihilation of Indians in India and the disappearance of Indian culture, the only valid purpose of the conquest could be the spread of the Christian faith. It was only with this in mind, according to him, that the pope had granted the patronage to Spain.[21]

To gain insight into the rationalizations of the day one should consider the questions then in discussion: "Are Indian beings gifted with intelligence or are they beings in between man and animal? Are they ordinary heathens or converts who have lapsed into heathendom? Noble savages or scabby dogs? The answers to these questions had an immediate bearing on colonial practice. They could serve to legitimatize it. For if Indians were rational beings, one could not justify their enslavement or the exaction of taxes. But, on the other hand, if they were savages, then their subjugation was largely justified. In this debate, Las Casas was virtually alone in defending the true humanity of the Indians![22]

Las Casas was always the advocate of peaceful coloni-

19. MacKay, p. 36.

20. J. M. van der Linden, *Heren, slaven, broeders; momenten uit de geschiedenis der slavernij* (Nijkerk: Callenbach, 1963), p. 75.

21. Mulders, pp. 193, 194; Dussel, pp. 82, 86.

22. Mulders, p. 194.

zation and pleaded for the human rights of the Indians. From 1550 to 1551, he was involved in a vehement dispute with J. G. de Sepúlveda, a dispute in which he favored the complete equality of the Indians with other people, whereas Sepulveda maintained—with the help of Aristotelian notions—that Indians as barbarians should submit themselves to the rule of the civilized Spaniards.[23]

Francisco de Vitoria, a Dominican theologian, seems to have been the first Spaniard who denied all political value to the papal donation. In his *Relection de Indis sive de jure belli Hispaniorum in barbares* (1546) he cited a long list of reasons which under certain hypothetical conditions justified the occupation and possession by Spain of the New World: resistance to the free course of the gospel, the protection of new Christians, the assistance owed to natives in a just-war situation, the free choice of indigenous tribes. But Francisco de Vitoria believed that, even if the faith had been proclaimed to the barbarians in an acceptable manner and they had nevertheless been unwilling to accept it, that still did not warrant judging them and taking their possessions.[24]

THE SPANISH CHRIST

In Cuzco, the ancient capital of the Incas, there is a church which goes back to colonial times. Above the door one reads: "Come unto Mary all ye that labour and are heavy laden and she will give you rest." According to John MacKay, this quotation is typical of the enormous role which Mary plays in the popular piety of Latin America and

23. Mulders, p. 195.
24. Francisco de Vitoria, *Le Cons sur les Indiens et sur le droit de guerre, 1538–1539* (Geneva: Droz, 1966), pp. 69, 70. Gutiérrez, in *The Power of the Poor in History* calls him a "centrist" theologian and charges him with being rather academic in his views (p. 196).

Spain.[25] "However much overshadowed by His Mother, Christ too came to America. Journeying from Bethlehem and Calvary, He passed through Africa and Spain on His long westward journey to the pampas and cordilleras. And yet, was it really He who came, or another religious figure with His name and some of His marks? Methinks the Christ, as He sojourned westward, went to prison in Spain, while another who took His name embarked with the Spanish crusaders for the New World, a Christ who was not born in Bethlehem but in North Africa." "This Christ became naturalized in the Iberian colonies of America, while Mary's Son and Lord has been little else than a stranger and sojourner in these lands from Columbus's day to this."[26]

And what, according to MacKay, is typical for the Spanish image of Christ? In answer to that question, he refers to the "sense of tragedy and a passion for immortality" which are the "warp and woof of Spanish popular religion" (p. 96). In this connection he cites the Spanish philosopher Jugo y Unamuno (1864-1936), who wrote a poem entitled *El Christo de Velazques* (1920). The famous image of the Christ of Velazques evidently occupied the same place in Unamuno's mind which Grünewald's picture of the cross with John the Baptist's finger pointed to the Crucified occupies in the thought of Karl Barth.[27]

Unamuno offers the following commentary on the

25. MacKay refers here (p. 94) to the Portuguese writer Guerra Junqueiro cited by Unamuno to the effect that the Spanish Christ was born in Tangiers. The idea is to suggest that the Spanish understanding of Christ was strongly influenced by Islam. Stated in this form I do not find the idea totally convincing but the question need not detain us here.

26. MacKay, p. 95.

27. MacKay, pp. 96, 148, 149; cf. Barth, *Church Dogmatics* I/2, p. 125; I/1, p. 126. Unamuno's most important work is called *The Tragic Sense of Life in Men and in Peoples* (London: Macmillan, 1921). He has been influenced by William James and Søren Kierkegaard as well as by Spanish mystics.

crucified Christ of Velazques, the recumbent Christ of Palencia *(Iglesia de la Cruz)*: "This Christ, immortal as death does not rise again. Why should he? He awaits nought but death. . . . This Spanish Christ who has never lived, black as the mantle of the earth, lies horizontal and stretched out like a plain. . . ." "In Spanish religion, Christ has been the center of a cult of death . . . . The dead Christ is an expiatory victim" (p. 98). The striking thing is that "the details of His earthly life are of slight importance and make relatively small appeal."[28]

In the Spanish conception of Christ "He is regarded as a purely supernatural being, whose humanity, being only apparent, has little ethical bearing upon ours. This docetic Christ died as the victim of human hate, and in order to bestow immortality, that is to say, a continuation of the present earthly, fleshly existence. The contemplation of His passion produces a sort of catharsis . . . in the soul of the worshipper, just as in the bull-fight, an analogous creation of the Spanish spirit, the Spaniard sees and feels death in all its dread reality in the fate of a victim. The total sensation intensifies his sense of the reality and terribleness of death; it increases his passion for life" but not in the sense of a craving for regeneration but for immortality. He partakes of communion, "not to become better" but "for private ends." "The Sacrament increases life without transforming it."[29]

This Spanish Christ who was brought and transmitted to Latin America is a Christ who was known especially as an infant in the arms of his mother and as a corpse on his mother's lap. For the latter one may recall the well-known depiction of Michelangelo, his Piéta in Rome. The mother presides over "his helpless childhood and tragic fate." The virgin mother, "by not tasting death, became the Queen of Life." It was this Christ and this Mary who were brought to

28. MacKay, pp. 97, 98.
29. MacKay, pp. 98, 101.

America. "He came as Lord of Death and of the life that is to be; she came as Sovereign Lady of the life that now is."[30]

It can be illustrated, by means of numerous Latin American depictions of Christ, that this is the Christ who was brought to this continent. Spanish missionaries pictured him as tragic Victim, bruised, ashen, bloodless; "blood-streaked images, twisted Christs that struggle with death and recumbent Christs that have succumbed to it."[31]

According to MacKay, it was precisely that Christ of the popular Spanish religion (the "Spanish Christ") who was "naturalized" in Latin America. Especially striking in this image is the absence of the history of his entire life. "As regards his earthly life, He appears almost exclusively in two dramatic roles—the role of the infant in his mother's arms, and the role of a suffering and bleeding victim. It is the picture of a Christ who was born and died, but who never lived. The great formative and decisive period of Jesus' life between helpless, unthinking infancy and His virile resolution to die with the untold suffering this entailed, is strangely passed over" (p. 110).

The humanity of Christ has exerted little appeal on Latin American worshipers. The reason is "they have known no Christ save one whom they could patronize" as infant and as suffering victim. "Christ is patronized in the elaborate Nativity festival at Christmas time, and again in the somber festivities that mark the course of Holy Week" (p. 111). In Latin America, Jesus Christ has functioned as a kind of catharsis, an emotional valve, but he has not been regarded as ethically significant. Latin American worshipers have had an "exclusive interest in Christ's meaning for death and immortality" which "has led them to ignore The One who . . . told men how to live. 'Follow me!'"

30. MacKay, p. 102.
31. MacKay, pp. 96, 97.

This sculpture of the crucified one by the Peruvian artist Edilberto Merida strongly resembles the figure of an executed guerilla warrior. This depiction became especially well-known after it was used on the dust jacket of the American edition of *A Theology of Liberation*, the book by liberation theologian Gustavo Gutiérrez.

"The vision of the Risen Christ . . . has been no less dim than that of the historical Jesus. . . . A most extraordinary thing has happened: Christ has lost prestige as a helper in the affairs of life. He lives in virtual banishment, while the Virgin and the saints are daily approached for life's necessities." "The Virgin is the real divinity of popular religion."[32]

How Christ was viewed by Latin Americans can best be illustrated by existing images of him, and in how his suffering is commemorated and observed. Just as in Spain, in Latin America processions are held during Holy Week, featuring horrible scenes filled with collective masochism. People drag heavy crosses through the street, turning the suffering of Christ into the cult of their own death and burial. But there is no Resurrection at the end of their Holy Week. Present-day testimonies stemming from the popular catholicism of Brazil show that faith in Jesus is not experienced as challenging; it is not a faith transforming heart and mind, producing hope and joy; rather, it is a kind of mystical repetition of one's own sad and disturbed existence.[33]

CHRIST AS LIBERATOR

It is against this background of the image of Jesus as it was transmitted by or came along with the Spanish conquistadores and was subsequently assimilated through a centuries-long process of interiorization in Latin America, that one must understand the image of Jesus depicted by the so-called theologians of liberation in Latin America today. Miguez Bonino prefers to speak of "theology in a context of liberation." In the movements of liberation in the

32. MacKay, pp. 111-13.
33. Cf. Galeano, p. 62; Luis Alberto de Boni, *Kirche auf neuen Wegen.* Diss., University of Münster, 1974, quoted by J. B. Metz, *Glaube in Geschichte und Gesellschaft* (Mainz: Matthias-Grünewald-Verlag, 1978), p. 123.

Third World he sees the liberating action of Yahweh and
Jesus Christ.[34]

The Columbian Everardo Ramirez Toro has written a
fifth gospel in which Jesus is transposed into a Latin-
American context as follows:

Some fragments:

> After Jesus was born in Macondo, during the presidency of
> Mr. Nixon, a number of astrologers from distant lands arrived
> in the capital of the empire Moneyland with the question:
> "Where is he who was born the Liberator of the people? For
> we have seen his star in the heavens and have come to make
> his acquaintance." When Nixon heard this, he was troubled
> and all the exploiters with him. Assembling all the civil,
> religious, and military leaders he inquired of them where the
> Liberator of the people was to be born. They told him: "In the
> village of Macondo, for so it is written by the prophets: 'And
> you, o Macondo, border region, you are by no means least, no
> less than all the capital cities of the world; for from you shall
> come a leader who will be the Liberator of the people."
>
> Then Mr. Nixon took the astrologers aside and from their
> information he discovered when the star had appeared. And
> he sent them to Macondo and said: "Go there and find out
> as much as you can about the child and when you have
> found him come and tell me because I also want to become
> acquainted with him." In those days came John Allende,
> called the forerunner of the liberation. . . .
>
> John Allende wore overalls with a leather belt around his
> waist. His meals consisted of rice and bananas, like the meals
> of peasants and factory workers. From all directions people
> came to hear him speak about the great changes which were
> about to come and how God would punish the exploiters of
> the people, and to listen to him demanding a change of heart.
> And all who had a change of heart he baptized by pouring
> water over them as a sign of liberation.
>
> Many came with a truly repentant heart but there were

34. Cf. Bussmann, p. 26.

also those whose hearts were full of venom—they came just
to escape the punishment predicted. These were the political
and religious leaders who oppressed the people. To them
John Allende spoke thus: "You brood of vipers! Do you
really want to escape the wrath of God? Then show some
sign of real repentance! And do not fool yourself by saying
over and over: 'We will be saved. After all, we confess the
traditional doctrine of the Catholic church.' I can tell you
with certainty: The axe is laid to the root of the tree, and
every tree that does not bear good fruit will be cut down and
thrown into the fire. . . ."

In the middle of the feast Jesus all of a sudden stood by
the church entrance and spoke with extraordinary
eloquence. The reactionary priests and the agents of the
regime said to each other furiously: "How can he know so
much about our problems when he has never studied at a
university." Jesus said: "The Good News of liberation is no
invention of my own but it has been taught to me by God,
the Father-of-the-people. God has said: 'Love your neighbor
as yourself' but you do not do what the law says: quite the
contrary, being stronger, you oppress the weak." He saw
certain agents of the Security Service who were standing in
the crowd to spy on him, and he said to them: "Now I ask
you—why do you men want to kill me?" They answered:
"You are crazy. Who wants to kill you?" Jesus answered:
"The only reason you want me dead is that I preach to you
love and equality and fraternity and I demand that you stop
exploiting people. . . ."

After this Jesus turned his face toward the capital of the
land and proceeded to go there. And when he was quite
close, he sent one of his followers to say to an old friend of
his, a simple man from among the people: "My friend, lend
me your donkey because I need it to enter the city." This was
done to fulfil a prophecy which says: "Tell the oppressed
masses: Look, here comes your Liberator, meek and defense-
less, seated—not in an armored limousine with bullet-proof
windows as the oppressors of the people ride in, nor in huge
processions—but seated on an ordinary donkey, an animal
that is used to hard work and to the whip." So his followers

went on their way and brought him the donkey. They laid
their coats on it and Jesus mounted the animal. As Jesus
came closer to the city, increasing numbers of people joined
him; the crowd grew into an enormous mass of people, slum
dwellers, laborers, students, taxi drivers, curiosity-seekers
and spies. The common people waved their handkerchiefs
and the branches they tore from the trees and whatever they
had available, shouting enthusiastically: "Long live our
leader! Long live he who has come to liberate us from the
oppressors in the name of God, the Father-of-the-people!
Long live our liberator. . . !"

As a result of certain incidents in the cathedral the religious leaders, by mounting a huge campaign through the
press, the radio, and TV, put pressure on the civil and
military authorities to finally arrest Jesus. Still, there was
much division in the land over this issue. Some said: "There
is no doubt he is the Liberator!" But others said: "He is a
subversive and a professional agitator!" Some ultra-rightist
groupings wanted to take him captive and sent a contingent
of police to him. But the policemen returned to their boss
empty-handed. When he asked: "Why didn't you put hand-
cuffs on him and bring him here?" they answered: "We
never heard anyone speak like that man."

Their superiors said: "You have let that subversive fellow
talk you out of it. Have you seen any of the higher-ups or
anyone in the church hierarchy who believed in him? But
these stupid people believe everything and anything."

After Jesus had talked at length about his ideas concerning liberation he said to his followers: "You know, don't you,
that in a few days the elections will be held and that the Son
of the people will be murdered?"

Then the authorities again met with the advisors of the
CIA and they decided to "liquidate" him, as that is called
in their jargon. Still, they agreed not to have it done during
the elections to avoid arousing the people who followed
him.[35]

35. E. R. Toro, *Het Zuid-Amerikaanse evangelie van de bevrijding*
(Amersfoort: De Horstink, 1978), pp. 18-20, 57, 58, 64, 65, 72.

Two theologians in Latin America who have displayed a strong preoccupation with Christology need to be mentioned here. First is the Brazilian theologian Leonardo Boff, who in 1972 wrote "the first cohesive Latin American Christology"[36] entitled *Jesus Christ Liberator: A Critical Christology for our Times.* The other book on Jesus Christ which became well known is that of Jon Sobrino, *Christology at the Crossroads: A Latin American Approach.*[37]

It may be that the reader, upon first scanning these books, will ask what is peculiarly Latin American about these "images" of Christ. After all, these authors prove to be quite familiar, and to tie in closely, with the European studies in the field of Christology. Peculiar to the various liberation theologies of Latin America, however, is that in their search for Jesus they are not led primarily by a theoretical, historical-exegetical interest, but by a practical one. Their concern is to discover the political dimension of Jesus' historic action, and of faith in him. The passion for liberation, which "is surging like a wave across the whole of Latin America, has become the hermeneutical key for the return to Jesus."[38]

It is Boff's purpose to make clear that the adoration of Jesus Christ and the mission to proclaim him as Liberator, as well as reflection on and the praxis of our faith in Christ, occurs in a socio-historical context which is characterized by domination and repression. The essential question one needs to ask, in his view, is who and what interest is being served by a certain "doctrine of Christ." The "Christology" of Jesus as Liberator finds itself in opposition to a Christology which supports "the whole process of colonization and domination: "The suffering and dying Christs of Latin

---

36. Bussmann, p. 43.

37. Jon Sobrino, *Christology at the Crossroads: A Latin American Approach* (Maryknoll, NY: Orbis, 1978).

38. Bussmann, p. 43.

American tradition are Christs embodying the 'interiorized impotence of the oppressed' (Assman). The Virgin pierced with a sword of sorrow personifies the submission and domination of women." The Christology of liberation takes the side of the oppressed.[39]

It is of great importance to note that over against "the doctrine of Christ" as it has been passed down and is usually held, a doctrine in which the life of Jesus seems to limit itself to the moments of his birth and death, here the historical Jesus is brought to center stage. The focus of this study is the entire active life and ministry of Jesus. The fact that this is the case has to do with the view that there is a structural correspondence between the situation prevailing in Jesus' days and that in which people live in South America. Boff and those who think like him constantly have in mind the concrete sociopolitical situation of Latin America. Latin American Christology, says Boff, gives priority to "the historical Jesus" over "the Christ of faith." What this means is something different from what Europeans might think. In the European "quest for the historical Jesus" the question was what were Jesus' own words and what had been structured and put into Jesus' mouth by the early church. But those are not the questions raised in the theology of liberation.[40] The difference, according to Jon Sobrino, is that European theology is related to the first phase of the Enlightenment (justification "before the bar of reason"), and the theology of Latin America is oriented to the second phase: changing reality.[41]

Latin American theology is not interested in that first-mentioned "quest." It assumes and starts out from the

39. Leonardo Boff, *Jesus Christ Liberator* (Maryknoll, NY: Orbis, 1978), pp. 264, 271.
40. Bussmann.
41. Sobrino, pp. 33ff., 348 ff., and *The True Church and the Poor* (London: SCM, 1985), pp. 10-15.

European studies on this point. Nor do confessional differences in this respect play much of a role.

Its interest is and remains practical in nature: theological reflection from within the social context of Latin America. This manner of speaking about Jesus and Christ is entirely at the service of a renewed Christian, and ecclesial, praxis. It would be doing these theologians an injustice to suggest that they would be willing to surrender their "faith" in Christ. The authors are priests who stand squarely in the liturgical tradition of their church. *The liberation of Jesus Christ is not so much a doctrine which is preached as a praxis which seeks to be realized.* Liberation theologians take for granted, as it were, the traditional confession concerning Jesus Christ. But they are in process of articulating a new interpretation of that traditional confession: Jesus Christ the Liberator.[42]

In the Christology of Jon Sobrino, this emphasis on the historical Jesus is especially strong and he develops it from within the Latin American situation of oppression, injustice, and exploitation. It is founded in the historical Jesus and in the history of the pain and suffering of a people.[43]

The only way to come to know Jesus is to follow him in the reality of his own life, to identify oneself with the interests for which he gave himself in his own day, and to try to establish his kingdom in our midst. Christian praxis is the only possible way to gain access to Jesus.[44] Following Jesus is the condition for knowing God (Jer. 22:16). Sobrino mentions two reasons for beginning with the historical Jesus: (1) There is correspondence between the Latin American situation and the time of Jesus; not only is there similarity between two situations of poverty and exploitation, but the themes

42. Bussmann, pp. 142-44.
43. Sobrino, pp. 12, 13.
44. Sobrino, pp. 34, 35.

also coincide. (2) The early Christian churches were not founded on imagined Christologies but on the witness of people who claimed they had seen the Risen One.[45]

According to Boff and Sobrino, "each generation of people brings a new Parousia of Christ because in each age he receives a new image." "In the experience of the faith of many Christians in Latin America" today "Jesus is seen and loved as the Liberator." "Latin America is not much interested in clarifying people's understanding of such traditional problems as transsubstantiation, the hypostatic union in Christ, and the relationship between divine and human knowledge in Christ." "Theological clarification of that sort does not seem to have any direct repercussions" for the social sphere. It is Sobrino's aim rather to put emphasis "on those Christological elements that serve to constitute a paradigm of liberation . . . or to highlight practical ways of understanding and realizing it, e.g., the socio-political activity of Jesus and the obligation to follow in his footsteps." "The aim of studying Jesus' intention is to pave the way for 'effective collaboration' with him." "The Kingdom of God expresses man's utopian longing for liberation from everything that alienates him, factors such as anguish, pain, hunger, injustice, and death, and not only man but all creation."[46]

To the Christ of faith, the resurrected Lord, says Sobrino, "we can gain access . . . through some sort of direct intentional act: e.g., a profession of faith, a doxology, a prayer, or cultic worship." However, as the gospels make clear, "we cannot gain access to the historical Jesus that way . . . We gain access to him only through a specific kind of praxis, which the Gospels describe as the 'following of Jesus,' or 'discipleship.' "[47]

45. Sobrino, pp. 12, 13.
46. Sobrino, pp. 34-37.
47. Bussmann, pp. 44-45.

Over and over in Latin American theologies of liberation, those two realities, that of one's own historical situation and that of Jesus' time, are related to each other. "If the death of Jesus and indeed death in general is not taken seriously—as reality—then discourse on God becomes idealistic and alienating." In Latin America the death of God is experienced as "the death of the other," of the Indian and the peasant.[48] Christian spirituality cannot limit itself to the mysticism of the cross but has to be a following of Jesus on the road in which he himself traveled.

The risen Lord is never disembodied. Today Jesus is always united with the people who are his body. He is continuously in search of his body (John 10:16: "I have other sheep, that are not of this fold; I must bring them also"). "These 'sheep' are the Indians. They belong to Christ. Accordingly no one can say he or she loves or worships Christ while at the same time separating from Christ the sheep that belong to him". . ."The repression of the Indians makes their free approach to Christ impossible". . ."A Christ cut off from his Indians is a gnostic being, a bodiless phantasm, a mystification of Christ—not the true Christ, risen and alive, whose new life consists precisely in being united to his Indians. "Through his proclamation of the perfect liberation of the human being the risen Christ appears as victor over the *whole* power of death."[49]

In sum, the concern of the Latin American theology (or Christology) of liberation is to understand Jesus as the liberator. Its interest extends to the whole of Jesus' life, to everything he did and said during his public ministry in the concrete historical situation of the first century. It places a strong accent on the "imitation" of Jesus, but not in the exclusive "spiritual" sense of the Imitatio Christi of Thomas

48. Bussmann, p. 115.
49. Bussmann, pp. 123, 124.

à Kempis: the concrete actions involved in going the way of
Jesus are the condition for learning to know his truth.

All this is intended to counterbalance the image of
Jesus in which he appears as the helpless infant in the arms
of his mother, or as the dead victim on her lap ("Pietá"). It
is a form of opposition to a Christology which is focused
only on Good Friday, and not on Easter, a Christology which
only offers to the poor a possibility, by the celebration of
Good Friday, of learning to bear one's own suffering, but
offers no opening toward the gospel of the resurrection to a
new life that is meant to begin now.

This representation of the crucifixion was made by Gloria
Guevara, Solentiname.

The Ethiopian church is one of the most ancient Christian churches in Africa. This representation of the wedding at Cana is an example of modern Ethiopian folk art.

IV 1. THE BLACK CHRIST

Lament For Dark Peoples

I was a red man one time,
But the white men came.
I was a black man, too,
But the white men came.

They drove me out of the forest.
They took me away from the jungles,
I lost my trees,
I lost my silver moons.

Now they've caged me
In the circus of civilization,
Now I herd with the many—
Caged in the circus of civilization.

Langston Hughes

THIS chapter, which is divided in three parts, first deals, in conjunction with the dramatic history of the blacks (slave trade), with the "white Christ" as well as with the "black Messiah" professed both in the United States (J. Cone, G. Wilmore) and in southern Africa (Canaan Banana).

The second part of this chapter relates particularly to the African continent itself, and treats the indigenous African religious background as well as the stages by which Jesus penetrated Africa (in the New Testament period, the Ethiopian; the ancient churches of Nubia and Ethiopia; the Christ transmitted by Western missions, both Protestant and Catholic). An attempt is made to sketch how Jesus is perceived in the so-called independent churches, and how African theologians try to construct their own African Christologies.

In the third part we consider how the Herrnhuters (Moravians) brought Christ to Suriname, as well as how the Creoles of Suriname "received" this Christ (Kwakoe and Christ).

JESUS AND THE SLAVE TRADE

Philip Potter, former secretary general of the World Council of Churches, relates how his ancestors were brought as slaves from West Africa to the West Indies on a ship called "Jesus." "The love of Jesus was . . . preached by white slaveholders who brought us into slavery in ships bearing names like 'The good ship Jesus,' a black man from North America tells us.[1]

The Portuguese, who built forts in Africa and specifically in Mombasa, Kenya, gave to one of them the name *Fort Jesus*.[2]

One cannot offer a clearer illustration than that provided by this nomenclature of how the name of Jesus was

1. D. Savramis, *Jezus overleeft zijn moordenaars* (Baarn: Ten Have, 1974), p. 123; George Cummings, "A North American Minority Answer"; cf. B. Dadié, *Patron de New York* (Paris: Prévence africaine, 1964), p. 263.
2. Noel Q. King, *Christian and Muslim* (New York: Harper & Row, 1971), p. 33.

misused and betrayed—and still somehow "transmitted." In the very same period in which voyages were made to the Americas, the African coast was explored, colonized, and conquered. The slave trade was bound up with the conquest and exploitation of the Americas. When the Indians proved unsuited for work in the plantations, the need arose for importing black manpower from Africa.

Angola, for instance, served as the supply base for the Brazilian slave trade.[3] A triangular trade pattern emerged. Cheap goods were brought from Europe to Africa; slaves from Africa to the Americas; and sugar and cotton back to Europe.[4] Over four centuries of slave trade, an estimated ten to twelve million captives arrived in America alive. Two million or more did not survive the ocean passage. The total loss is estimated at twenty million people.[5]

The slave trade involved a large-scale human hunt on behalf of plantation slavery, in which the Portuguese, soon to be followed by the English and the Dutch, were the pioneers.[6]

The consequences of this trade were horrible. African society was disrupted, since it was especially young workers who were taken away. Internal tensions between African tribes were exploited as an excuse for taking people captive. It was the tactic of the Portuguese, for example, to wage war with the aid of native bands against neighboring tribes.[7]

As a rule the slave traders, though Christians, seemed

3. R. Oliver and J. D. Fage, *A Short History of Africa* (Penguin Books, 1962), p. 128.

4. B. Davidson, *Africa in History, Themes and Outlines* (New York: Macmillan, 1968), p. 189.

5. Davidson, pp. 178-94. K. L. Roskam, *De kolonisatie van Afrika* (Bussum: Unieboek b.v., 1973), p. 9, claims that the slave trade up to the beginning of the nineteenth century cost Africa ca. 100 million people.

6. C. R. Boxer, *The Golden Age of Brazil, 1695-1750: Growing Pains of a Colonial Society* (Los Angeles: Univ. of California Press, 1962), p. 2.

7. Oliver and Fage, p. 128.

to have no "problems" with their occupations. John New-
ton, author of "How Sweet the Name of Jesus Sounds," was
a slave trader in his youth.[8]

As a result of the slave trade, Catholic missions in
Mozambique, for example, declined. It was the missionaries' attitudes toward slavery which had a negative effect
upon their mission.[9] "Unfortunately, the extension of the
slave trade soon began to loom larger in Portuguese aims
than the creation of a Christian state in Africa." "By the end
of the eighteenth century Christianity was but a memory"
in the Congo.[10]

With respect to the African continent as a whole, therefore, the process of Christianization was in a state of stag-
nation as a result of the slave trade till the beginning of the
nineteenth century. It remains a deep mystery that despite
this betrayal of Christ, Christ was nevertheless "transmitted" to black people, even on board those slave ships!

Criticism of the slave trade, though rare, is not totally
missing before the nineteenth century. In a letter written
to the Capuchins in 1682, the prefect of the Propaganda
Fide lamented the slave trade in the Congo.[11] A certain J. G.
Haafner (1755–1809), a one-time seaman and the author of
travel tales, in a book entitled "Inquiry into the usefulness
of missionaries and missionary societies," spoke of the
disgrace of slavery and claimed that no persons would
accept the God of those who exercised tyranny over
them.[12] However, it did happen, a fact which is and remains a riddle.

8. King, p. 37.
9. A. Mulders, *Missie-geschiedenis* (Bussum: Paul Brand, 1957),
p. 324.
10. Oliver and Fage, p. 126.
11. Mulders, p. 322.
12. J. M. van der Linde, "Honderd jaar zendingswetenschap in
Nederland," *Nederlands Theologisch Tijdschrift* 31 (1977): 233.

THE WHITE CHRIST AND THE BLACK MESSIAH

It is the descendants of the black slaves who were shipped from Africa to the Americas, who in recent decades in the United States became conscious of the extent to which the Jesus transmitted to them was, and is increasingly, made "white." In opposition to this development they champion the "blackness" of Jesus. The "whiteness" of Jesus is meant not only in the literal and external sense of the word but also and particularly in the figurative sense. Gayraud S. Wilmore has pointed out how in Western art the depiction of Jesus becomes ever whiter and paler. It seems to him the intent was to change Jesus from a Semite into an Aryan. His dark hair was rendered light, his dark eyes blue. "The Aryanization of Christ according to the logic of color symbolism commenced when white Europeans began to come into close contact with darker races."[13]

Black theology, which developed in the United States beginning in the 1960s, opposes a "white theology" which created a God in the image of the Western white man. That is the foundation, as black theologians see it, of the ideology of the Christian West and of the oppression which blacks and other nonwhites have experienced. To counter the Christian faith which identifies God with the dominant white culture, black theology poses a God who identifies with the oppressed of every race and nation and is present in their suffering, humiliation, and death. Black theologians speak of a black Messiah, this oppressed and murdered God, who arose to give life and hope to all who are oppressed. The black Messiah, the oppressed man of God, is seen in the faces of poor and oppressed black people. His death and resurrection, as it occurs in their rising to new life

13. G. S. Wilmore, "Black Theology," *International Review of Missions* 63 (1974): 228.

and power, is the meaning of the gospel of liberation. Jesus Christ can be de-Americanized without losing his essential significance as the incarnate Son of God. Black theologians see the oppressed and murdered Messiah rise in actual symbols, which differ from those of white Westerners.[14]

James Cone, the black theologian who first thrust black theology into the public arena, wrote: "The 'raceless' American Christ has a light skin, wavy brown hair, and some- times—wonder of wonders—blue eyes. For whites to find him with big lips and kinky hair is as offensive as it was for the Pharisees to find him partying with tax-collectors. But whether whites want to hear it or not, *Christ is black, baby*, with all of the features which are so detestable to white society. To suggest that Christ has taken on a black skin is not theological emotionalism.... Thinking of Christ as non- black in the twentieth century is as theologically impossible as thinking of him as non-Jewish in the first century."[15]

What is the significance of Nicea (the Council of Nicea, A.D. 325, which declared that Christ is of the same substance as the Father), and Chalcedon (the council in 451 which stated that the two natures of Christ, the divine and the human, are without division or separation, and without confusion or change), for those who know Jesus not as a thought in their heads but as savior and friend?[16] Accord- ingly, Cone says, he began once more to listen to the heart- beat of black life as reflected in the songs and speech of blacks. This Cone does especially in his book *The Spirituals and the Blues*. According to him "the Spirituals are the story of the black strivings for earthly freedom rather than the

14. G. S. Wilmore and J. H. Cone, *Black Theology, A Documentary History, 1966-1979* (Maryknoll, NY: Orbis, 1979), pp. 140, 141; cf. Theo Witvliet, *A Place in the Sun* (Maryknoll, NY: Orbis, 1985), pp. 43-85.

15. J. H. Cone, "The White Church and Black Power," in Wilmore and Cone, pp. 116, 117.

16. J. H. Cone, *God of the Oppressed* (New York: Seabury, 1975), p. 5.

otherworldly projections of hopeless Africans who forgot about their 'homeland'. " In the Spirituals "Jesus is understood as the King, the deliverer of humanity from unjust suffering. He is the comforter in time of trouble, the 'lily of the valley' and 'the bright morning star.' . . . The Spirituals are silent on theological speculations" (are not all songs and hymns?—*A. W.*). "Jesus was not the subject of theological questioning. He was perceived in the reality of the black experience." The Spirituals are unequivocal in their reference to the divinity of Jesus. "Language about the Father and the Son became two ways of talking about the reality of the divine presence in the slave community." Christ's life, death, and resurrection are central. "His death was a symbol of their suffering." Jesus is present in that suffering because "he is their friend and companion in slavery." The Spirituals do not speak only about what Jesus has done and is doing for blacks in their enslavement. They also interpret him as holding the keys to Judgment. "Jesus is God himself breaking into man's historical present and transforming it according to divine expectations."[17]

Cone stresses that Jesus Christ must be confessed in terms of his past, present, and future. "We can truly know Jesus' past and its soteriological significance only if his past is seen in dialectical relation to his present presence and his future coming."

"In our analysis of the past history of Jesus we cannot ignore his present soteriological value as the Lord of our present struggle. The same is true for his future coming." "The vision of Christ's future that breaks into their slave existence radically changes their perspective on life." "Unless black theologians can demonstrate that Jesus' blackness is not simply the psychological disposition of black people

17. J. H. Cone, *The Spirituals and the Blues* (New York: Seabury, 1972), pp. 15, 47, 50, 53, 55, 57.

but arises from the faithful examination of the Christological sources (Scripture, tradition, and social existence),
sources which illuminate Jesus' past, present and future, we
lay ourselves open to the white charge that 'the black Christ'
is an ideological distortion of the New Testament for political purposes." "He is black because *he was a Jew*." The
assertion "Jesus is black" can be understood "when the
significance of his past Jewishness is related dialectically to
the meaning of his present blackness." "The Jewishness of
Jesus located him in the context of the Exodus, thereby
connecting his appearance in Palestine with God's liberation of oppressed Israelites from Egypt" (Isa. 42:6, 7). The
cross of Jesus is God's reversal of the human situation. The
elected one takes the place of Israel as the Suffering Servant
and so manifests "the divine willingness to suffer in order
that humanity might be fully liberated." "The cross represents the particularity of divine suffering in Israel's place."

The resurrection means that God's identification
"with the poor in Jesus is not limited to the particularity
of his Jewishness but applicable to all who fight on behalf
of the liberation of humanity in this world." Cone admits
that he realizes that "blackness" as a Christological title
may not be appropriate in the distant future or even in
every human context in the present. But in his view "this
was no less true of a number of New Testament titles like
'Son of God' and 'Son of David' " and other descriptions
of Christ used in the course of Christian history. The
validity of a title is decided, however, by whether at a
specific time in history "it points to God's universal will
to liberate particular oppressed people from inhumanity."
The blackness of Jesus, accordingly, is "not simply a statement about skin color but rather the transcendent affir-
mation that God has not ever, no not ever, left the
oppressed alone in their struggle. He was with them in
Pharaoh's Egypt, is with them in America, Africa, and

Latin America, and will come in the end of time to consummate fully their human freedom."[18] Says Cone: "There is no truth in Jesus Christ independent of the oppressed of the land—their history and culture." Christ "is an event of liberation, a happening in the lives of oppressed people struggling for political freedom."[19]

THE "BLACK MESSIAH" IN AFRICA

Black theology is found not only in the United States but also in Africa, especially in those parts which used to suffer, or still suffer, under the heel of white racism or white domination. That is very much the case in South Africa,[20] of course, and in Zimbabwe, formerly Rhodesia. In Zimbabwe, the Rev. Canaan Banana, at one point its president, some time ago wrote *The GOSPEL According to the GHETTO*. For too long, he believes, the ghetto masses have had "the Gospel of pie in the sky forced down their throats." But God wants to meet us in our strength, not in our weakness. It is Canaan Banana's hope, above all, "that those who are disenchanted will awaken anew to the fact that the God we adore" is not dead or weak but alive and active in creating and recreating human beings and their environment.[21]

18. Cone, *God of the Oppressed*, pp. 130, 131, 133, 134, 135, 137.

19. Cone, *God of the Oppressed*, pp. 33, 34.

20. Cf. J. Tödt Hrsg., *Theologie im Konfliktfeld Südafrika, Dialog mit Manas Buthelezi* (Munich: Kösel-Verlag, 1976); A. Boesak, *Farewell to Innocence, A Social-Ethical Study on Black Theology and Black Power* (Kampen: Kok, 1976).

21. Canaan Banana, *The GOSPEL According to the GHETTO* (Geneva: W.C.C., 1977), p. 5.

He articulates his own creed as follows:

Statement of Belief

The Christian Faith motivates man,
To aspire for the fullness of life,
In the HERE and NOW.

The Gospel of Jesus Christ,
Is a WHOLE Gospel to the WHOLE man.
It seeks to redeem man in his totality,
It does not compartmentalise him.
The Gospel of Jesus Christ,
Has the power to heal,
The bleeding wounds of the
Moral, social, economic,
And political ills of our age.
The Gospel of Jesus Christ,
Affirms the worth of every man,
It exposes the dominant myth of
Divine racism.
It advocates the brotherhood,
Of all men as the only hope of the world.[22]

He offers the following example of the people's creed:

The People's Creed

I believe in a color-blind God,

Maker of technicolor people,
Who created the universe
And provided abundant resources
For equitable distribution among all his people.

I believe in Jesus Christ,
Born of a common woman,
Who was ridiculed, disfigured, and executed,

22. Banana, p. 7.

Who on the third day rose and fought back;
He storms the highest councils of men,
where he overturns the iron rule of injustice.
From henceforth he shall continue
To judge the hatred and arrogance of men.

I believe in the Spirit of Reconciliation,
The United body of the dispossessed;
The communion of the suffering masses,
The power that overcomes the dehumanizing forces
    of men.
The resurrection of personhood, justice, and equality,
And in the final triumph of Brotherhood.[23]

The following adaptation of the Lord's Prayer is also his:

The Lord's Prayer

Our Father which art in the ghetto,
degraded is your name,
Thy servitude abounds,
Thy will is mocked,
as pie in the sky.

Teach us to demand,
our share of gold,
forgive us our docility,
as we demand our share of justice.

Lead us not into complicity,
deliver us from our fears.

For ours is Thy sovereignty,
the power and the liberation,
for ever and ever. . . , Amen.[24]

23. Banana, p. 8.
24. Banana, p. 9.

"Jesus Christ is the conqueror;
by his resurrection he overcame death itself,
by his resurrection he overcame all things:
he overcame magic,
he overcame amulets and charms,
he overcame the darkness of demon-possession,
he overcame dread.
When we are with him,
we also conquer."

African Christian song from the Transvaal

THE AFRICAN RELIGIOUS BACKGROUND

IN addition to the two great world religions, Christianity and Islam, Africa also knows of African religion, rather, religions. Although African religion(s) also have their own adherents, it remains important to observe that this peculiar African religiousness has attached itself in one way or another both to Christianity and Islam, so that it may even be asked which has had the greater influence on which. Lamin Sanneh has pointed out that both in the African forms of Christianity and those of Islam the African has

African crucifix
In his poem "I am an African," Gabriel Setiloane speaks of the crucified Christ as an African, burned by the sun, naked, and in pain. In this depiction of the crucifixion, an unknown African artist represents Christ as smiling, despite the suffering he is experiencing—just as in the Negro spiritual the words "Nobody knows the trouble I have seen" can be sung in conjunction with the "Glory Hallelujah."

exerted and still exerts a large measure of influence on the shape of both religions.[1]

With reference to this peculiarly African element, it has been repeatedly pointed out how disinclined in his thought patterns the African is toward individualism and how he truly experiences his humanity only in fellowship with others.[2] The African theologian Gabriel Setiloane has made the point that, whereas for the Westerner the statement "I think therefore I am" ("Cogito ergo sum," Descartes) is and has become typical, for the African the truth is: "I am because we are."[3] The African is very conscious of his ties to the community, of belonging to an "extended family," one that consists of the living and the dead. This latter conviction implies that for the African person those who have preceded him or her in death are not really altogether dead, meaning that they continue to play a role in the fortunes or misfortunes—depending on whether they are pleased or displeased—of their descendants. Those ancestors are called the "living dead." Only the most important ancestors live long in the memory of their descendants and so continue to be involved in their lives helping them, or haunting them if something in the conduct of their progeny displeases them. Thus, sickness or accidents can be traced back to their intervention or involvement, and the living are expected regularly to enter into contact with their brother-ancestor by way of prayer and, if necessary, ritual sacrifices to calm him down.[4]

1. Lamin Sanneh, *West African Christianity; the Religious Impact* (Maryknoll, NY: Orbis, 1983).

2. Kofi Appiah-Kubi, "Jesus Christ: Some Christological Aspects from African Perspectives," in John S. Mbiti, *African and Asian Contributions to Contemporary Theology* (Geneva: W.C.C. Ecumenical Institute, 1977), p. 56.

3. G. M. Setiloane, "Christus heute bekennen aus der afrikanischen Sicht von Mensch und Gemeinschaft," *Zeitschrift für Mission* 2 (1976): 24.

4. Charles Nyamiti, "Christ as our Ancestor: Christology from an African Perspective," *Service* 4 (1981): 1.

The dead are assumed to be friendly and well disposed toward their living family members, though they may inflict disasters upon them when they are angry. And when this happens the living may, by prayers and sacrifices in the form of food and drink, make amends. On their part, the living expect care and protection from their ancestors.[5] The royal chief may mediate between the living and the dead. And the ancestors, for their part, are able to mediate between the living and God.[6] In African society, the occurrence of illness is often attributed to the violation of a taboo or to the machinations of evil spirits or, at times, of ancestors who are upset. The one can injure the other by magic or witchcraft. A neighbor may have uttered a curse; the evil eye may be to blame. The victim is not necessarily the guilty party. It may be that a relative committed the misstep. The question which then becomes paramount for the African is: "Why me? Why does this happen to me?"

For that reason demand for and concern about healing are of central significance. The medicine man or *nganga* may be called in to help in order, by way of divination and "revelation," to track down the guilty. According to N. W. Turner, the two things mentioned constitute the double role of the *nganga*. The first, divination, means that he will expose hatred and spite as the causes of sickness and misfortune while, with the second, "revelation," he unveils another reality in which these things do not exist in their present form. He provides a vision of a society as it should be.[7]

5. Charles Nyamiti, "Christ as our Ancestor: Christology from an African Perspective," *Service* 5 (1982): 10.
6. Appiah-Kubi, p. 56; cf. John S. Mbiti, *Introduction to African Religion* (London: Heinemann, 1975); Mbiti, *African Religions and Philosophy* (London: Heinemann, 1969).
7. Cited by J. M. Schoffeleers, "Christ as the Medicine Man and the Medicine Man as Christ: A Tentative History of African Christological Thought," *Man and Life, a Journal of the Institute of Social Research and Applied Anthropology* 8, 1 and 2 (1982): 19.

Precisely because sickness is frequently "social" in nature and is a function of a disturbed harmony in society, the *nganga* can play an important role in the restoration of that harmonious order.[8]

In the life of native Africans, so-called "rites of passage" are important as transitional customs observed at the times of birth, initiation, marriage, and death. To become a complete person, incorporated in African society, one has to submit to the necessary rites.[9]

JESUS' ADVENT IN AFRICA

Jesus was in Africa even before the rise of Christianity. After all, the Holy Family had to flee to Egypt and, according to tradition, stayed there for six months. Right into the present guides are prepared to show the place where they are alleged to have lived. The Ethiopian who is mentioned in Acts 8, and who was baptized by Philip the evangelist, was presumably an African and possibly a citizen in the kingdom of Meroë. The beginnings of the church in Egypt are traced back to St. Mark, of whom the Coptic patriarch called himself the successor. As a result of the work of two brothers who suffered shipwreck in the Red Sea, Frumentius and Aedesius of Tyre, Christianity gained a foothold in Ethiopia. Frumentius brought about a link with the Coptic church in Egypt, and in the sixth century Christianity expanded to Nubia.

From the seventh century on, the origination and expansion of Islam caused a weakening of Christianity and Islam began to bar the expansion of Christianity. In the

8. Appiah-Kubi, p. 62.
9. For a detailed description of an initiation rite, cf. A. Droogers, *The Dangerous Journey: Symbolic Aspects of Boys' Initiation* (The Hague: Mouton, 1980).

Middle Ages, at the time of the crusades, when Nubians attempted a linkup with "Western" Christians, Nubian Christianity sustained severe damage and fell prey to aggression from Islam.[10]

In the western part of North Africa—once the location of the churches of Tertullian, Cyprian, and Augustine—the church had already declined before the expansion of Islam. When North Africa ceased to be "Latin" it also virtually ceased to be Christian, at least in the sense that no indigenous church remained in existence. From the side of Africans, however, the continuing relevance of, say, Cyprian, for present-day theological discussion has been pointed out.[11]

New contact between Christianity and Africa came about at the time of the great commercial voyages first launched by the Portuguese. The missionary expedition of 1490, customarily considered the first missionary venture, succeeded in the Congo. In 1491 the king and the queen were baptized and given the names of the Portuguese king and queen, Joan and Eleonora. From then on their son, Mvemba Nzinga, was called by his baptismal name, Don Alfonso, and beginning in 1507 he became the great Christian king of the Congo (d. 1534).[12]

An earlier section already demonstrated how in time the slave trade had a most negative effect on the expansion of Christianity in Africa, one which lasted until the nineteenth century. Once the slave trade was abolished in the West, the Arabs continued it for the sake especially of domestic slavery—slaves serving in households or harems

10. B. Davidson, *Africa in History, Themes and Outlines* (New York: Macmillan, 1968), pp. 99-121.
11. E. W. Fashole-Luke, "Footpaths and Signposts to African Christian Theologies," *Bulletin de Theologie Africaine*, 3 (5): 23.
12. Mulders, *Missie-geschiedenis* (Bussum: Paul Brand, 1957), pp. 203, 204.

in countries like Egypt, Arabia, and Persia. Their number is estimated at approximately 400,000 a year.[13]

It was David Livingstone (d. 1873) who, by his travels and journals, exposed this slave trade worldwide. He aimed to clear the way for "Christianity and trade" because in his opinion the trade in human beings could only be stopped by regular trade relations and the development of agriculture.[14]

When Western missions again focused on Africa, Protestants were on the scene before Catholics, and among Protestants the Baptists were the first (1792). Catholics followed later, with the White Fathers, under the later Cardinal Lavigerie, playing a special role beginning in 1868.

The really massive expansion of Christianity south of the Sahara took place after the beginning of the nineteenth century, a century sometimes called "the Age of Missions." This expansion continues to the present, so much so that it has been predicted that by the end of this century African churches will outnumber those in Europe.

Missionaries to Africa established settlements both on the coast and in the interior, gathering around themselves the small groups, often of freed slaves, who were to be their first converts.[15] Some historians have pointed out that a distinction has to be made between the missionaries who served from the beginning till 1884—people like Livingstone—and those after 1884, the year of the Congress of Berlin when Africa was divided between the great powers of Europe, the so-called "scramble" for Africa. The earlier missionaries were usually learned persons who carefully

13. Mulders, p. 417.

14. J. van den Berg, "Een open pad voor handel en Christendom," in *Christus-prediking in de wereld: Studiën op het terrein van de zendingsweten-schap gewijd aan de nagedachtenis van Professor Dr. Johan Herman Bavinck* (Kampen: Kok, 1965), pp. 63-90.

15. Oliver and Fage, *A Short History of Africa* (Penguin Books, 1962), p. 179.

studied the language and customs of the countries in question. Missionaries of the later phase as a rule lived further away from the Africans, followed a Western lifestyle with the aid of imported materials and goods, often resided in "compounds," had to rely on interpreters, and could count on the support and protection of colonial administrators.[16]

The role of the later missionaries often seemed alien to the Africans. One reason was that many of them, in bringing the gospel, showed very little interest in the African cultural and religious background. Modern African literature reflects and satirizes this state of affairs. We shall cite one example here, without claiming it as representative for all missionaries. Beti Mongo, a writer from Cameroon, in his *De arme Christus van Bomba*, describes the experiences of a missionary on a two-week safari, as seen through the eyes of a faithful Catholic "mission-boy." The central figure is the father-superior, Drummont, who has lived and labored in Cameroon some twenty years.

The novel begins as follows:

> I do not believe it's blasphemy. . . . O no! It makes me happy even to think it was perhaps Providence itself, the Holy Spirit, who whispered into my father's ear: "Be sure to tell them that Jesus Christ and father-superior are one and the same," when the little ones of our village looked intently at pictures of Jesus and, struck by his resemblance to father-superior (the same beard, the same robe, the same cord around his middle), cried out: "But Jesus Christ looks just like father-superior!" And my father assured them that Jesus

16. Louisa Ngo Tappa, *Christian Mission and African Culture*, pp. 29-31. Oliver and Fage, p. 180, state that had "full-scale European intervention been delayed fifty years," a much larger part of Africa would have belonged culturally to the world of Islam. This, of course, is one of the many "ifs" of history. One could at least question this hypothesis on the ground that there are also examples of the reverse. The interventions of Europe at the time of the crusades were a factor in the ruin of Christianity in Nubia.

and father-superior were indeed one and the same. Since
that time the children of my village call father-superior
"Jesus Christ." In time the missionary reached a deadlock in
his work and became unsure about his mission, which is the
reason he finally returned to France. "Why should he come
back? We cared so little for him; it was as if he did not belong
to us, because he was not really one of us."[17]

JESUS IN THE SO-CALLED "INDEPENDENT CHURCHES"

Since as a rule the churches which resulted from mission
work were negative toward African customs, there arose
in many parts of Africa the so-called "independent
churches," a name, incidentally, which these churches
themselves do not use. The word "independent" refers to
the fact that they separated themselves from the so-called
mission churches. At the moment there are an estimated
7,000 of these independent churches in Africa. In South
Africa alone there are 3,000. About 25 percent of all African
Christians are considered members of these churches. The
number of adherents of the separate independent
churches varies from only several to thousands, or, in
some cases, to more than a million people. One of the
largest independent churches is that of the Kimbanguists
in Zaire. Simon Kimbangu, an African from the "Belgian
Congo" with a Baptist background, in 1921 felt called by
the voice of Christ. After a public ministry of only a few
months, he was arrested by the Belgian authorities and put
in the jail where he remained till his death in 1951, a period
of 30 years!

Today "the church of Jesus Christ on Earth through the

17. Beti Mongo, *De arme Christus van Bomba* (Bussum: Het Wereld-
venster, 1980), p. 15.

Prophet Simon Kimbangu" is one of the largest churches in Zaire. Its membership is estimated at five million and is presently led by Simon Kimbangu's son Joseph Diangienda. In 1969 the church was admitted to the World Council of Churches.[18]

Independent churches are distinguished in various ways. The usual distinction is between an Ethiopian type and a "spirit" or prophetic type. The first designation is intended to stress the authentically African origins of African Christianity, those preceding the arrival of mission churches. In this context the tendency is to quote the Scripture which refers to Ethiopia: "Let Ethiopia hasten to stretch out her hands to God" (Ps. 68:31). In the independent churches of the Ethiopian type the life and doctrine of the church do not differ much from those of the mission churches, but the emphasis is on the African leadership. In the "spirit" churches the "spirit" or the prophetic dimension is central. They form a fellowship of believers like the early Christian churches and have a center, which they call Zion, which is considered a concrete part of the realized kingdom of God on earth.[19]

"I AM AN AFRICAN"

Christianity came to Africa in a series of distinct phases. The result was that one cannot speak of a single, homogeneous image of Christ which was brought to Africa. The "Christ of the Portuguese" is different from that which washed ashore, so to speak, with Aedesius and Frumentius in Ethiopia.

---

18. A. Hastings, *African Christianity: an Essay in Interpretation* (London, 1976), p. 1; M. L. Martin, *Kimbangu: an African Prophet and his Church* (Oxford: Blackwell, 1975).

19. B. Sundkler, *Bantu Prophets in South Africa* (New York: Oxford Univ. Press, 1961²).

Perhaps what the African Christian thinks of Jesus
Christ today as opposed to the white Christ brought to him
by others can best be reproduced by quoting a poem by the
African theologian Gabriel M. Setiloane: "I am an African."
It shows the typical African response to Jesus Christ.

> They call me African:
> African indeed am I:
> Rugged son of the soil of Africa,
> Black as my father, and his before him;
> As my mother and sisters and brothers, living and gone
>   from this world.
>
> They ask me what I believe . . . my faith.
> Some even think I have none
> But live like the beasts of the field.
>
> "What of God, the Creator
> Revealed to mankind through the Jews of old,
> the YAHWEH: I AM
>
> Who has been and ever shall be?
> Do you acknowledge Him?"
>
> My fathers and theirs, many generations before,
>   knew Him.
> They bowed the knee to Him
> By many names they knew Him,
> And yet 'tis He the One and only God
> They called Him:
> UVELINGQAKI:
>   The First One
>   Who came ere ever anything appeared:
> UNKULUNKULU:
>   The BIG BIG ONE,
>   so big indeed that no space could ever contain Him.
> MODIMO:
>   Because His abode is far up in the sky.
> They also knew Him as MODIRI:
>   For He has made all;

and LESA:
The spirit without which the breath of man cannot be.

But, my fathers, from the mouths of their fathers, say
That this God of old shone
With a brightness so bright
It blinded them . . . Therefore . . .
He died himself, UVELINGQAKI,
That none should reach His presence . . .
Unless they die (for pity flowed in His heart).
Only the fathers who are dead come into His presence.

Little gods bearing up the prayers and supplications
Of their children to the GREAT GOD . . .
"Tell us further you African:
What of Jesus, the Christ,
Born in Bethlehem:
Son of Man and Son of God
Do you believe in Him?"

For ages He eluded us, this Jesus of Bethlehem, Son of
Man:
Going first to Asia and to Europe, and the western sphere,
Some say He tried to come to us,
Sending His messengers of old . . . But . . .
They were cut off by the desert and the great mountains
of Ethiopia!
Wanderers from behind those mountains have told
Strange tales to our fathers,
And they in turn to others.

Tales of the Man of Bethlehem
Who went about doing good!
The theme of His truths is now lost in the mouths of
women
As they sissed their little children and themselves to sleep.

Later on, He came, this Son of Man:
Like a child delayed He came to us.
The White Man brought Him.

He was pale, and not the Sunburnt Son of the Desert.
As a child He came.

A wee little babe wrapped in swaddling clothes.
Ah, if only He had been like little Moses, lying
Sun-scorched on the banks of the River of God
We would have recognized Him.
He eludes us still this Jesus, Son of Man.

His words. Ah, they taste so good
As sweet and refreshing as the sap of the palm
   raised and nourished on African soil
The Truths of His words are for all men, for all time.

And yet for us it is when He is on the cross,
This Jesus of Nazareth, with holed hands
   and open side, like a beast at a sacrifice:
When He is stripped naked like us,
Browned and sweating water and blood in the heat of
   the sun,
Yet silent,
That we cannot resist Him.

How like us He is, this Jesus of Nazareth,
Beaten, tortured, imprisoned, spat upon, truncheoned,
Denied by His own, and chased like a thief in the night.
Despised, and rejected like a dog that has fleas,
for NO REASON.

No reason, but that He was Son of his Father,
OR . . . Was there a reason?
There was indeed. . . .
As in that sheep or goat we offer in sacrifice,
Quiet and uncomplaining.
Its blood falling to the ground to cleanse it, as us:
And making peace between us and our fathers long
   passed away.
He is that LAMB!
His blood cleanses,
  not only us,
  not only the clan,

not only the tribe,
But all, all MANKIND:
Black and White and Brown and Red,
All Mankind!

HO! . . . Jesus, Lord, Son of Man and Son of God,
Make peace with your blood and sweat and suffering,
With God, UVELINGQAKI, UNKULUNKULU,
For the sins of Mankind, our fathers and us,
That standing in the same Sonship with all mankind
    and you,
Together with you, we can pray to Him above:
FATHER FORGIVE.[20]

According to Gabriel Setiloane, the task of African theology is to grapple seriously with the question of Christology: "Who is Jesus?" How did he become the supreme human manifestation of the Divinity, the Messiah of Judaism and the *Christos* of Hellenistic Christianity? What does "Messiah" or "Christos" mean in the African context? According to Setiloane, an authentic African Christology must be sought somewhere in the area of the African *Bongaka* and in the possession of individual persons by the Divinity. The term *Bongaka* refers to a traditional African doctor, often disparagingly called "witch-doctor" or "jujuman."[21]

Hastings remarks that in his view, despite the African concern for contextualization among African theologians like Mbiti and Nyamiti, Idowu and Fashole-Luke, Tshibangu and Agossou, their theology remains remarkably controlled in language and methodology by Europe and the academic centers where they studied.[22] In contrast with this, Hastings

20. G. M. Setiloane, "I Am an African" in *Mission Trends No. 3*, G. H. Anderson and T. F. Stransky, eds. (Grand Rapids: Eerdmans, 1976), pp. 128-31.

21. Kofi Appiah-Kubi and Sergio Torres, eds., *African Theology En Route* (Maryknoll, NY: Orbis, 1979), p. 64.

22. Hastings, p. 58.

refers to the theology of the African independent churches, which, in the conviction of M. L. Daneel, have developed a "meaningful Christology." "Their experience of Christ in the rich ritual life of their churches, and their perception of his presence, though it may not always be fully articulated, provide clues to a somewhat obscured but nevertheless presupposed and very real Christology."[23] The independent churches have a kind of "oral theology" in which "not the definition but the description, not the explanation but the story, not the book but the people, not the summa theologiae but the song, are central."[24]

This "independence" was already manifest before the nineteenth century in the church founded by a girl named Vita Kempa. Central in that church was a "black" Christ who takes the side of oppressed Africans. In 1706 Vita Kempa was burned to death in the Congo.[25]

It is said of the prophet Shembe that he is a revelation of Jehovah among the Zulus, as Jesus was among the Jews. This Shembe, in addition to being the messiah of the Zulus, is also regarded as one who will restore the ancient splendor of the Zulu kingdom. His son and successor, Galilee Shembe, does make Christ central in his church, although in the liturgy and the hymns it is Shembe and not Christ who is the central figure.

The question raised from time to time in this connection is whether in present-day independent churches certain of these church founders or leaders have not usurped the place of Jesus. This has been suggested, for instance,

---

23. M. L. Daneel, "Towards a Theologia Africana? The Contribution of Independent Churches to African Theology" *Missionalia* 12 (Aug. 1984): 77.

24. Appiah-Kubi and Torres, pp. 64, 65.

25. F. J. Verstraelen, "Afrika en zijn godsdiensten" in *Wat geen oog heeft gezien* (Hilversum: Catholic Radio Broadcasting, 1981), p. 38.

with regard to people like Shembe. But currently the view prevails that the so-called black messiahs do not obstruct the position of the biblical Christ but rather somehow illuminate his life.[26] It is considered more accurate, for example, to compare Simon Kimbangu with Simon of Cyrene, who assisted Jesus on the way to Golgotha by carrying the cross, or to see Shembe function as the mask of the black messiah by which he can be recognized by the Zulus.[27]

AFRICAN CHRISTOLOGICAL TITLES

In 1967 the well-known Kenyan theologian John Mbiti made the statement that African concepts of Christology do not exist.[28]

In December 1974, at a consultation of African theologians in Accra, Ghana, Dr. E. W. Fashole-Luke of the University of Sierra Leone, West Africa, remarked that "there are no signs that Christological ideas are being wrestled with by African theologians," an aspect, he said, which "needs to be given top priority."[29]

Ten years after Mbiti's statement Kofi Appiah-Kubi of Ghana observed that there was very little literature on the subject of African Christology.[30] In 1979 Gabriel Setiloane (Botswana) declared that the task given to African theology today is to work hard and thoroughly at such a Christology:

26. Daneel, p. 77.
27. Daneel, p. 78.
28. J. S. Mbiti, "Some African Concepts of Christology" in G. F. Vicedom, ed., *Christ and the Younger Churches* (London: S.P.C.K., 1972), p. 51.
29. E. W. Fashole-Luke, "The Quest for African Christian Theologies," in Anderson and Stransky, p. 148.
30. Appiah-Kubi, "Jesus Christ," p. 55.

Who is Jesus? What does "Messiah" or "Christ" mean in the
African context?[31]

Since these initial "calls" for an African Christology
were issued, a number of designs have been proposed, be it
tentatively, which seek to bring to the fore the African
Christological "titles of majesty."[32] Some of these titles are
as follows:

Christ as "Victor"

Basing his views on a study of sermons delivered in the
Church of the Lord (Aladura) in Nigeria, John Mbiti reports
that the people in these churches display a special interest
in the principal events of the life of Jesus, such as his birth,
baptism, death, and resurrection, as well as the resurrection
of those who have been incorporated in the body of Christ.
Jesus is viewed, above all, as the conqueror. He fights
against and triumphs over the powers of the devil, disease,
hatred, fear, even death itself.

When the question is posed why to African Christians
Christ as victor should be so attractive, the answer given is
that the African Christian is very much aware of the various
powers at work in his life and environment: spirits, magic,
witchcraft, "fear, anxiety, sickness, diseases, the power of
evil and the greatest of them all, death."[33]

John Mbiti explains this orientation and preference in
the light of African anthropology. God has created the child

---

31. G. M. Setiloane, "Où en est la théologie africaine?" in Kofi
Appiah-Kubi, ed., *Libération ou adaptation? La theologie africaine s'interroge*
(Paris: Librairie Editions l'Harmattan, 1979), p. 81; cf. P. Stadler, "Ap-
proches christologiques en Afrique," *Bulletin de Théologie-africaine* 5 (Jan./
June 1983): 35-51.

32. Cf. Ferdinand Hahn, *The Title of Jesus in Christology* (London,
1969).

33. Mbiti, "Some African Concepts," p. 54.

and given him or her to the community. It is up to the community to incorporate that child in human society. To that end a person has to experience "the rites of passage": birth, initiation into adulthood, marriage, and death, the passage to the world of the ancestors. According to Mbiti, African Christians are particularly drawn to the birth, baptism, and death of Jesus because these events highlight Jesus as a complete human being who has undergone the necessary rites of passage. Hence, also their interest in the genealogies in Matthew 1:1-17 and Luke 3:23-38.[34]

Jesus meets all the criteria for a complete, "corporate" member of society. He is a complete, perfected, whole adult, and responsible human being. Because he is a perfect human being he dies in order to complete his identification with man. "The cross is not a sign of shame and humiliation: but a symbol of completeness as far as the human life of Jesus was concerned." This interpretation, says John Mbiti, does not "deprive the death of our Lord of its sacrificial and soteriological consequences. These consequences derive from, rather than lead to, the cross." An ordinary human being called Jesus died. The "Christian" difference arises from the resurrection, the event "by which the Christian faith stands or falls." That which happened before Easter is an experience all people share. That which happens after Easter constitutes the uniqueness of the gospel.[35]

Christ as "Chief"

One of the titles which African theologians have proposed for Christ is that of "chief," a title originally proposed by Western missionaries. Says Paul de Fueter: "We preach Christ who is really the chief, the king for Africa. He is the

34. Cf. Appiah-Kubi, "Jesus Christ," p. 56.
35. Mbiti, "Some African Concepts," pp. 56, 57.

ruler who comes and in whose presence all is forgotten, with whom one is secure forever."[36] This title is called an unfortunate choice, however, because "chiefs" are or were people who are often far removed from their people and only accessible through middlemen.[37] J. S. Pobee even goes so far as to call the analogy of Christ as "chief" dangerous because it is a theology of glory without the theology of the cross. The chief-analogy denotes authority and power derived from other ways than the way of suffering.[38]

Christ as "Ancestor"

Another title which is sometimes used for Jesus is that of the great or greatest "ancestor." (*Nana* in the Anka language.) According to J. S. Pobee, Jesus is *Nana* like the other illustrious ancestors; he is the incomparable judge, superior to the other ancestors because he is the closest to God. To say that Jesus is *Nana* is to let his standards reign supreme in personal orientation, in the structures of society, in the economic processes, and in the political arena. It means personal and social justice. An African who affirms that Jesus is *Nana* should also relate that message to the issues of human and social justice in Africa and the rest of the world.[39]

The African Catholic theologian Charles Nyamiti has offered a further dogmatic elaboration of this idea by attempting to show that, analogically speaking, God the Father is the ancestor of the Logos, the descendent of the

36. A. Shorter, *African Christian Spirituality* (Maryknoll, NY: Orbis, 1978) p. 66.

37. Shorter, p. 66.

38. J. S. Pobee, "Toward Christology in an African Theology," in his *Toward an African Theology* (Nashville: Abingdon, 1979), p. 97.

39. Pobee, p. 98.

Father. God is our Father and ancestor through Christ. By his incarnation and redemption Christ is our ancestor. His being our ancestor resembles the relationship existing between a dead African individual and his or her brothers and sisters. Nyamiti has in mind the type of ancestry existing between dead brothers and their siblings in a family, because this type of ancestry most resembles the analogy between Christ and us. Christ, then, is the brother-ancestor. The comparison is between African brothers, dead and alive, and Christ's relationship to people.

His divine-human status makes him potentially the brother and mediator of any human being whatever, whether Adamic in origin or not. Nyamiti insists, however, that Christ's sonship to the Father is radically different from our sonship to that same Father. Closely tied in with his hypostatic union is Christ's salvific mediation. Christ as ancestor is the pattern for human conduct. He is the inner source and vital principle of the Christian life. Christ not only imparts physical or material benefits to his brothers but especially spiritual goods, the greatest of which is himself, the benefit of eternal salvation. As human being Jesus is our natural brother in Adam. As the God-man he is the brother-ancestor of all human beings.

Charles Nyamiti further states that the complete resurrection of the total Christ still has to come. His ancestorship has not been fully effectuated. His saving activity will reach its fulfillment in the appearance of Jesus Christ *(parousia)* when the cosmos receives the fullness of the fruits of his resurrection. This, says Nyamiti, shows the intimate connection existing between Christ's incarnation, ancestorship, and redemption.[40]

40. Nyamiti, "Christ as Our Ancestor," *Service* 5 (1982): 8, 9, 12, 13, 14, 21.

Christ as "Healer"

Especially in the independent churches faith-healing practices play an important role. The most frequent answer
given to the question why someone has joined a church is:
"For a long time I was sick. I tried all sorts of treatments but
without results. I received the advice to go to such-and-such
a prophet. I did that and now I am better. Praised be the
Lord."[41] These faith-healing practices have such great influence it is understandable that "Christ is best understood as
healer, wonder-worker and protector against evil powers
. . . An authentic African Christology should be sought in
the area prepared by the traditional healer."[42]

"The prophetic Independent Churches place the paradigm of Christ as 'the *healing inganga*' in sharper relief than
any other church in Africa." "The healing prophet himself
personifies the liberating and healing ministry of Christ. He
preaches about Christ the Healer during services preceding
healing activities." "In him," says Daneel, "the *nganga* tradition is continued on the one hand but radically converted
into a Christian form on the other. In his laying on of hands,
his prayers, his distribution of holy water and other symbols
of God's healing power and in his dramatic exorcism of evil
spirits, Christ emerges in the African world as the One who
cares, protects, restores, and who banishes fear."[43]

Schoffeleers, in a fascinating essay in which he has
been aided by a description of the Bwiti cult of Gabon and
the Mbona cult of Malawi, has written about Christ the
nganga as the paradigm par excellence for an African
Christology.[44]

41. Appiah-Kubi, "Jesus Christ," p. 63.
42. Daneel, pp. 83-84.
43. Daneel, pp. 84, 85.
44. J. M. Schoffeleers, see note 7 above; he is especially inspired by
an article by R. Buano Kibongi: "Priesthood," in *Biblical Revelation and*

The excitement implicit in the idea of using the *nganga* as model for the image of Christ lies precisely in the fact that the *nganga* or medicine man was viewed by Protestant and Catholic missionaries alike as the adversary of Christ,[45] one reason why some Africans are skittish toward such a practice, and comparable perhaps to the objection to using the title "chief."

In his conclusion, Schoffeleers states that Christian officebearers as well as Christ himself can be designated as *nganga*, but also the reverse is true: *ngangas* also assume Christian and christological attributes. On the one hand, there is pressure to arrive at new forms of human community: the *nganga* is transformed into Christ; on the other there is the urge to adapt traditional forms: Christ is transformed into *nganga*.[46]

African Belief, Kwesi A. Dickson and Paul Elligworth, eds. (London: Lutterworth Press, 1969), pp. 57-74.

45. Daneel, p. 84.

46. Schoffeleers, p. 19.

IV   3. CHRIST IN SURINAME

SURINAME is sometimes called the most West African country in the Americas.[1] A large number of black Africans from Suriname have meanwhile gone to live in the Netherlands. In the past the Dutch were among the first (for a time the very first) of the slave traders who carried off black slaves from West Africa to Suriname and returned from there with a shipload of sugar.

People have often thought that as a result of the trans-Atlantic voyage to the West the blacks would also have left behind their religion and culture. Just as this applies to other blacks in other parts of the Americas, so it is becoming clearer and more generally known that they took along ancient traditions, and that these traditions have lived on. Among the things they brought with them were belief in spirits, ancestor-worship, prayers, dances, knowledge of black and white magic. They had their own priests and medicine men. Voodoo is the name for the popular religion of the blacks who have their own religious concepts and rites and who later in the Americas and the West combined them with Catholic and Protestant ideas.[2]

1. J. M. van der Linde, *Heren, slaven, broeders; momenten uit de geschiedenis der slavernij* (Nijkerk: Callenbach, 1963), pp. 100, 101.
2. J. M. van der Linde, *Ballade van de slavenhaler* (Nijkerk: Callenbach, 1963), p. 24.

The so-called Winti, the Afro-American religion practiced in Suriname, has survived at a deep level among the Creoles, next to and within Christianity. It is and has been for centuries an "institutionalized" religion which at night attracts many people in the districts and in areas around the capital.[3]

CHRIST AND HERRNHUT

In order to answer the question which image of Christ was brought to Suriname one must say a few words about the Herrnhuter ideas concerning Christ, because it was the Herrnhut missionaries who transmitted the gospel of Jesus to Suriname. The heart of their theology was determined by the theology of Count von Zinzendorf (1700-1760), whom Karl Barth has described as the only genuine "Christocentric" of the modern age.[4]

The hymns of Zinzendorf were always centrally focused on the Savior and his merits: God can be known to people only in his incarnate Son, Jesus Christ. The emphasis in his theology is on Jesus' "Blood and Wounds."

The suffering Savior, who had made a powerful impression on Zinzendorf in his youth, led him to enthrone the Lamb of God as the real Creator, Sustainer, Redeemer, and Sanctifier of the universe. The same "Lamb of God" inspired him to proclaim his doctrine of Jesus' suffering as a universal theology in theory and practice, according to J. M. van der Linde.[5]

---

3. C. J. Wooding, *Winti, een 'Afro-Amerikaanse' godsdienst in Suriname* (Meppel: Krips Repro, 1972), p. 203.

4. K. Barth, *Church Dogmatics* IV/1, p. 683.

5. J. M. van der Linde, *Het visioen van Herrnhut en het apostolaat der Moravische Broeders in Suriname,* 1735-1863 (Paramaribo: Kersten, 1956), pp. 60, 61.

In the eighteenth century Zinzendorf saw himself facing two fronts: on the one hand, the rule of "reason" which ends in atheism, and on the other, the mysticism which is neglected in the institutional life of the church. In Zinzendorf's theology, says Van der Linde, the crucified Lord whom Grünewald had confessed and adored on the Isenheim altar two centuries before, came to life again in a most powerful way. Zinzendorf never ceased to speak and sing of the Lamb who bleeds. Over against the experiential Christianity of Pietism—with its nervous self-scrutiny, Zinzendorf posed the objectivity of the blood shed on the cross. It was a theology of the wounds of Jesus (cf. John 19:15-37), a following of the finger of John the Baptist on the Isenheim altar which always pointed toward the crucified Savior, wounded and bleeding.[6]

The focus for Zinzendorf is not the tragedy of human suffering in a most cruel world; it is the Son of God, incarnate for the redemption of the world from sin. That is how Zinzendorf sought to depict before the eyes of his contemporaries—Christians, heathens, rationalists, orthodox, pietists—the concreteness of the salvation of God in Christ. To be intelligible, this salvation must be proclaimed as something tangible and apprehensible.[7]

"The wound in Jesus' side," in Zinzendorf's preaching, was the most highly condensed and complex expression of the message of reconciliation and redemption. The depiction of the first convert of Herrnhut—that is, the first from among the nations—reproduces a person stretching out his hands to the wounds in Jesus' feet. An Indian is shown pointing to the wound in Jesus' side. On a painting of Jephta, the Indian evangelist in Barbice (ca. 1750), he is depicted preaching to his heathen compatriots, showing in

6. Van der Linde, *Het visioen van Herrnhut*, pp. 62, 65, 67.
7. Van der Linde, *Het visioen van Herrnhut*, p. 66.

the palm of his own hand the stigma of the nail that pierced it.[8]

True, Zinzendorf opened the eyes of the Brothers of the Herrnhut mission to the pluriformity of lands and cultures, as well as persons. But in his opinion "the message" could be everywhere the same. In matters of the heart there are no national differences.

> Oh! let us in thy nailprints see
> Our pardon and election free.[9]

In Zinzendorf's theology the Creator is the Redeemer. The name Jehovah receives an *interpretatio christologica*. In the *Litaney zu den Wundes des Lammes* (1747) the entire work of the three persons of the Trinity is related to redemption by Christ. It is striking how his theology has become Christology and in his Christology everything converges, as it were, on the point of the wounds—the suffering, death, and resurrection for the sake of reconciliation.

THE CHRIST BROUGHT TO SURINAME

To a large degree it was the Christ image of Zinzendorf which the evangelical Brethren brought with them to Suriname. The Christ preached in the colony was strongly colored by it. At one of the first visits of the Herrnhut missionaries the blacks were confronted with God as Jesus who gives his blood for people.[10]

8. Van der Linde, *Het visioen van Herrnhut,* pp. 67, 68.

9. Van der Linde, *Het visioen van Herrnhut,* p. 68; A. J. Lewis, *Zinzendorf, the Ecumenical Pioneer: A Study in the Moravian Contribution to Christian Mission and Unity* (London: SCM, 1962), p. 70, strophe 17.

10. We are using the interesting study by J. F. Jones, *Kwakoe en Christus; Een beschouwing over de ontmoeting van de Afro-Amerikaanse Cultuur en religie met de Herrnhuter zending in Suriname* (Brussels: n.p., 1981), p. 44.

In 1766 Dehne, a Herrnhut missionary, accompanied
by the brothers Stoll and Jones, pushed toward the Bush
Negroes of Saramacca on the Upper Suriname. Upon arrival, his first words to the *granman* (title of a chief among
Bush Negroes in Suriname) Abini have the central message
with which the Herrnhut of the eighteenth century sent its
messengers into the world: "That I loved the negroes and
wanted to speak to them about their Creator who shed his
blood for you and all men, who loves you and wants the
negroes to know this because they had not been told
before." The *granman*, responding to the words about the
Creator, asked whether he was the Grangado, that is,
whether he was the same one whom the Sarramaccans call
God (High God). Dehne then started his sermon by saying
that the God whom the Negroes call Grangado is named
Jesus Christ.

The first person baptized from among the Sarramaccan
tribe was the son of the *granman*. In the hut belonging to
Rudolph Stoll, who had gone out together with Dehne, he
saw a depiction of the crucified Christ. When he asked who
that was, Stoll answered: "It is a representation of the high
God (Grangado), the Creator of Heaven and Earth. He so
humbled himself and out of love for us became a human
being that on account of our sins he permitted himself to be
executed. Now he is causing you to be told that you must
give him your heart, and pray to him for the forgiveness of
your sins, then you will have it good with him without fail." [11]

Chief Abini related: "Gradually I learned to know
myself as a great sinner and experienced the power of the
blood of Jesus Christ, something I am familiar with to this
day." Thus, a concept till then unknown to the tribal religion, that of "great sinner," becomes highly charged as a
result of the work of the Herrnhut mission.

11. Van der Linde, *Het visioen van Herrnhut*, p. 168.

In 1777 a translation was produced of a harmonized version of the gospel passion-stories which left a specific imprint on the spirituality of many Suriname Christians. During the seven weeks of Lent, as this is known in the liturgical tradition of Protestant churches, this passion history was read to the people.

Every Good Friday there was a reading from this passion history, a practice which led to the idea of an annual repetition of the suffering and death of Jesus. Also, in the songs sung at the Moravian mission posts the suffering Jesus occupied a very important place.

> Lamb of God
> Thanks and praise to Thee are due;
> O accept our adoration
> For the blessings ever new.[12]

Songs and hymns were pivotal in the Moravian missionary enterprise. The Moravians used song as an important means of preaching the gospel among blacks in Suriname, since the sung word spoke, and still speaks, to the heart of the black man.

Just as James Cone has made this point with reference to the spirituals of the black slaves in North America,[13] so we learn here that in covert and symbolic ways songs were sung and games were played to protest the ill-treatment received at the hands of the slaveholder, and all in his presence.

A certain form of Negro song endemic in Suriname, the Doe, was always spiced with reference to the political and social life of the whites as well as to other free persons.[14]

However, a study made of these songs drew the fol-

---

12. A. J. Lewis, p. 63.
13. Cf. J. H. Cone, *The Spirituals and the Blues* (New York: Seabury, 1972).
14. Jones, pp. 21, 22, 25.

lowing conclusion. In comparison with the suffering, distress, and death of Jesus, the resurrection of Christ was celebrated little. It would seem that under Zinzendorf's influence Easter took second place to Good Friday.[15]

Van der Linde also asserts that the songs sung in the Suriname community of the Brethren were steeped in the passion-mysticism of Herrnhut and that the adoration of the wounds, the blood, and corpse of Jesus occupied a large place in earlier and later editions of the Song Book (Singi Boekoe). In other words, the songs sung in Herrnhut, in which the dominant theme was the Lamb who suffered and died, were kept for us among the blacks. The Jesus they got to see was the one of "O Sacred Head Now Wounded." In the song Jesus appeared to blacks as the Suffering Servant, as a lamb led to the slaughter, who "opened not his mouth." In the context of human suffering Jesus was not permitted to speak.[16]

"KWAKOE" AND CHRIST

What then is that religious world of the black Surinamese and how did it relate to Christ? This question is the subject of the dissertation by J. F. Jones already cited, entitled *Kwakoe en Christus.*

In this title "Kwakoe" stands for the personification of the black slave and his descendants, his Afro-American religion and culture.[17] In Suriname society the African Winti-religion has been preserved. The spiritual treasures of West Africa were adapted and made serviceable to the

15. R. E. Berggraaf, *Vo Singi a de switi; een kritische beschouwing over het Singi boekoe en het lied van Heernhut in Suriname* (a thesis at the Protestant Theological Faculty, Brussels, 1968); cited by Jones, pp. 25, 46.

16. Jones, p. 46.

17. Jones, p. 7.

demands of the Suriname environment, that is, a slave society.

In actual fact, this religion and Christianity often went hand in hand. It frequently happened that Jesus was added to the West African pantheon, accepted as one of the many good gods and spirits. Christ was quite often worshiped and addressed as one of the great ancestors, "the living dead."

The African, says Jones, reinterpreted his African legacy in a manner enabling him to utilize his philosophy of life to his own optimum advantage in the face of the ruling class of the plantocracy.[18]

In Suriname, reports Jones, all sorts of ritual actions designed to placate or adjure spirits—rituals which sometimes gave rise to crime—were regarded as "idolatry." In criminal law idolatry was listed as a punishable offense, a provision not abolished until 8 September 1971. But it was the colonial administration which obviously saw the religious background of the blacks as a potential danger which might incite them to disturb the colonial order.[19]

According to Jones, the Herrnhut missionaries proved more powerful than the gods of the blacks. The black man saw himself able, by virtue of the missionary presence, to help abolish these much-venerated and dreaded gods. To the minds of blacks the removal of images was a genuine liberation from specific oppressive powers under which they suffered. For their part, the missionaries believed that their actions constituted a victory of the gospel over the religion of the blacks. The result was that the blacks felt increasingly inferior to the whites. History shows, according to Jones, that though "Kwakoe" could be deprived of his external images, Christ did not thereby come to possess his entire house.

18. Jones, pp. 11, 12.
19. Jones, pp. 30, 31.

In Jones's judgment, the Christ transmitted to Suriname left the existing conditions of oppressive slavery virtually untouched, while the religious background of the African Surinamese was neglected or depreciated. He refers to the "colorless Jesus" (Helpiman) of the Herrnhut Brethren and to Herrnhut theology as a reduction of the gospel: "The Brethren of Herrnhut did not allow Jesus to say a single word of liberation about the dreadful slavery in which the blacks found themselves." The liberation celebrated in the hymns and church songs was a liberation into the hereafter. "In the case of songs of resurrection the condition of the negro in the slave colony is simply ignored. The thrust of those songs is that Jesus is victor over sin and that the power of sin was broken by the cataclysmic event of Jesus' resurrection. . . . The fact that the resurrection means life for human beings is a biblical given, but the fact that in their songs the Herrnhut missionaries forced Jesus to be silent about the slave existence of the negro is . . . not biblical. In their theory and practice Jesus did not openly choose sides for the oppressed person against his oppressors. . . . In the songs of the missionaries he never became a black Jesus who suffered with people and championed the cause of the black man. . . . Jesus was not the total Liberator, but the Lamb who suffered."[20]

Jones contends that because the religious world of the blacks was neglected and not properly appreciated a real confrontation between the biblical message and the religious world of the black man never happened. In Jones' opinion, the message of the Herrnhut missionaries was unable to touch the inmost essence of blacks, although what the missionaries brought them could possibly serve as a stimulus for the Surinamese to do their own thinking from within the biblical message.

20. Jones, pp. 40, 43, 46, 47, 51.

*   *   *

The image which Africans have formed of Jesus Christ can
be found in various parts of the world—Africa, the Americas, and in Suriname. It is an image bound up with the
dramatic and turbulent history of black people. Next to the
(continued) existence of the image of Christ conveyed by
the different missions, there is the Jesus who is viewed and
experienced by blacks, especially in North America and
southern Africa, as Liberator. The understanding and interpretation of Jesus Christ in the diverse African religious
context is still in an early stage. The challenge which
proceeds from this unique religious context has been perceived and is being opened up for discussion, but the designing of a uniquely African Christology still seems pro-
visional and hesitant. The so-called independent churches,
however, most emphatically bring to center stage the image
of Jesus Christ as "healer," the "physician of souls" *and*
bodies!

V 1. THE ASIATIC FACE OF CHRIST

> *In his representation of the Last Supper, the Bengal artist Jamini Roy (1887-1972) has depicted Christ with large staring eyes, sometimes called fish eyes and linked by some with fish, which have no eyelids, therefore never blink, and accordingly symbolize God's continuing watchfulness over the needs of his people.*

In this chapter we shall deal with the Asiatic face, or the Asiatic faces, of Christ. After a short account of the ancient churches of Asia, we shall say a few words about the "colonial Christ" brought to the Asian continent. After some reference to the preeminently pluralistic religious context of Asia (pt. 1), there will follow a discussion of some of the many Asian Christologies and images of Christ, particularly some Indian Christological designs. Specifically, we will consider the views of a Catholic (Raimundo Panikkar) and a Protestant (Stanley Samartha) theologian (pt. 2). In the concluding section we shall stop to consider, in light of the work of Jung Young Lee, a Korean theologian, how Jesus is understood in the context of Taoism.

Jesus came from Asia, West-Asia as it is sometimes called today. Asian Christians rightly make a point of this over against an image of Jesus Christ as a European, in which he is appropriated by Europeans as a Westerner or white man. It was not long after the church's beginnings that Christian churches appeared in all kinds of Asiatic countries. The most mission-minded church in the first centuries was the Nestorian church, which extended as far as China. In later centuries, however, this church disappeared from large areas of this continent, so that there is mention of an "eclipse" of Christianity in Asia.[1] In West Asia, or the Near East, these most ancient churches survive in the form of the so-called orthodox churches—the Syrian Orthodox (especially in Syria, Lebanon, and Turkey), the Nestorians or Assyrians (particularly in Iraq), the Maronites (Lebanon), and the Armenians.[2]

In the whole of Asia, where three-fifths of the entire world population is found, and three-fourths of the poor,[3] only two percent of the population is "Christian." Of these, the majority are found in the Philippines and Indonesia, two countries which seem to form an exception to the "rule" in Asia.[4]

Accordingly, whereas Latin America and sub-Saharan Africa can be regarded as largely Christian, that is not at all true of Asia. The question how Jesus is understood is, therefore, also a question concerning the relationship of Jesus Christ and the Christian church(es) to the religions of Asia. And then we are talking, inter alia, of the "great"

1. E. G. Browne, *The Eclipse of Christianity in Asia* (Cambridge: Cambridge Univ. Press, 1933).

2. Cf. my *Arabier en christen; Christelijke kerken in het Midden-Oosten* (Baarn: Ten Have, 1983).

3. Tissa Balasuriya, *Jesus Christ and Human Liberation*, Quest Series (1981; reprint, Colombo: Centre for Society and Religion), p. 93.

4. A. Pieris, "Towards an Asian Theology of Liberation: Some Religio-Cultural Guidelines," *Dialogue*, n.s. 6 (1979): 35; *Le Monde*, 30 October 1982, p. 9, mentions over 60 million Christians in Asia, 2.3% of the total population, and only 0.8% if Philippine Christians (83% of the Christian population) are subtracted.

religions, such as Hinduism, Buddhism, and Taoism, "soteriologies" which differ from the Christian.

Aloysius Pieris, the Asiatic theologian from Sri Lanka,
has written: "Hence our desperate search for the Asian face
of Christ can find fulfillment only if we participate in Asia's
own search for it in the unfathomable abyss where Religion
and Poverty seem to have the same common source: God,
who has declared Mammon his enemy" (Matt. 6:24).[5]

The same author has remarked in another place that
the church in Asia can only become the church of Asia if it
takes thorough account of the two great realities of Asia: its
poverty and religiosity. He asserts that the cause of the
failure of Christianity in Asia—referring particularly to the
later missions—must be sought in its association with that
mammon, meaning commercial and colonial exploitation,
and its refusal to enter into the monastic religiosity of what
he calls the "non-Christian soteriologies."[6]

THE COLONIAL CHRIST IN ASIA

The Christ brought by the missionaries was usually, though
not always, closely bound up with colonialism. As a rule, to
use an expression coined by Richard Niebuhr, it was (a) a
"Christ against culture and religion"[7] and (b) an oppressive
one at that.

(a) In the time of European ecclesiastical expansion the
"colonial" Christ was at odds with the religions—often
viewed as false—of the so-called Third World.[8] Not even

5. John C. England, ed., *Living Theology in Asia* (London: SCM, 1981),
pp. 175, 176.
6. Pieris, "Towards an Asian Theology," pp. 29, 36.
7. Cf. the final chapter VI, A.
8. So says A. Pieris, "Non-Christian Religions and Cultures in
Third World Theology," *Vidyajyoti* 66 (Apr. 1982): 167.

the work of Roberto de Nobili and Mattheo Ricci constituted an exception. Roberto de Nobili, the Jesuit who in 1605
pleaded for Christian participation in such Hindu-festivals
as Pongal, suggested that Christians cook their newly
harvested rice at the foot of the cross planted in the ground
for that purpose. His approach, however, was mainly
directed to making Christianity look externally the least
objectionable. He made no attempt to modify any part of his
theology, the tridentine theology of his time.[9]

In 1706 the first Protestant missionary, Bartholomew
Ziegenbalg, arrived in India. In his (imprinted) *Remarkable
Voyage* he wrote in this vein: "I do not reject everything they
teach but rather rejoice that long ago a small ray of Gospel
light began to shine among the heathen. If only the
European reader could see how far by the light of reason
they have come in the knowledge of God and the natural
order, and how, aided by their natural powers, they have
often by their sincere conduct put to shame many Christians, and also display a much greater effort toward the
future life!"[10] Such expressions of positive appreciation for
the "natural religions" and "rationality," however much
influenced by the insights of the seventeenth and eighteenth
centuries, found little support at the time. A. H. Francke
(1663-1727), undoubtedly reflecting the general attitude of
Western Christian missionaries over a long period of time
stated: "The missionaries were sent out to eradicate
heathendom in India, not to spread heathen nonsense over
all of Europe."[11]

(b) It is hard to deny that often an unholy alliance

9. J. R. Chandran, "Development of Christian Theology in India: A
Critical Survey," p. 159.
10. Chandran. (Unfortunately, not having this article at my dis-
posal, I could not reproduce the quotation directly but had to translate it
back into English from Dutch.—Trans.)
11. Chandran, p. 160. (A reverse translation as before.—Trans.)

existed among missionaries, soldiers, and merchants. It was a mercantile Christianity, which with the help of foreign colonial powers planted the cross in Asia.[12] "Catholics brought to Asia a Christ as understood by Spaniards, the Portuguese, and later the French, Italians, Belgians, and North Americans. The Protestants carried with them an Anglo-Saxon version of Christ."[13] Since Christ was brought to Asia in conjunction with colonialism, it is understandable, as a Catholic theologian from Sri Lanka has stated, that as a rule there was no criticism from this direction of the exploitation of the nations in question. European people spoke of a divine plan of "redemption," but what they brought was only a message of personal emancipation or deliverance. "Christology" was developed along individualistic lines. Jesus was interested in the renewal of the heart, not in social reform. Tissa Balasuriya further points out that theology was more oriented to the church than to Christ or even to God. In the nineteenth century the missionaries emphasized the relationship to Jesus understood as friend. Jesus was regarded as One who came to redeem the human race from original sin. He believes that almost the whole of Catholic life was built around such an individualistic notion of Jesus and Mary. In this connection he refers to the enormous influence of Thomas à Kempis, who in the very first chapter of his *Imitatio Christi*, dealt with "contempt for the world." Almost his entire attitude toward nature, world, life, and human love is negative. According to Tissa Balasuriya, by being so one-sided à Kempis was largely responsible for a well-intended but disastrous distortion of the image of Jesus Christ. "This whole combina-

---

12. A. Pieris, "Mission of the Local Church in Relation to Other Major Religious Traditions," *Sedos Bulletin* 82, 5 (Mar. 1982); 6 (Apr. 1982); 7 (May 1982): 127.

13. Balasuriya, p. 8. (A reverse translation.—Trans.)

tion of theology, spirituality, and devotion filled into the background of oriental feudalism, despotism and superstition and Western capitalism in its imperialistic phase."[14]

Tissa Balasuriya, like the liberation theologians of Latin America, points out how in such an interpretation Jesus' life and death is viewed more as an act of obedience to God than as the logical outflow of his personal choices, the choices Jesus made in the context of the society of his day. What gets lost in such a view is his love for people in their situations of oppression and the liberating process which resulted.[15]

Aloysius Pieris goes so far as to say that the various missions of today make the same mistake when, by way of massive development programs, they permit the churches in Asia to settle in Western oases—large establishments in private education, technology, or agriculture, financed with help from abroad. In this movement he sees a continuation of a missiology of "conquest" and "power" which in his opinion was characteristic of the colonial period.[16]

ASIATIC RELIGIONS

Before we further explore the images of Christ present in various parts of Asia, such as India and China, it is probably useful to comment on the religious-cultural boundaries of Asia. In this connection Aloysius Pieris has made reference to three things: (1) the linguistic heterogeneity of Asia; (2) the integration of cosmic and meta-cosmic elements in the religions of Asia; and (3) the overwhelming presence of non-Christian soteriologies ("soteriology" is the branch of theology that deals with salvation).

14. Balasuriya, p. 11.
15. Balasuriya, p. 9.
16. Pieris, "Towards an Asian Theology," p. 36.

On the subject of (1), he distinguishes seven large language zones in Asia: the Semitic, the Ural-Altaic, the Indo-Iranian, the Dravidic, the Sino-Tibetan, the Malay-Polynesian, and the Japanese. Language, to Pieris, is a distinct new way of experiencing truth. This implies that linguistic pluralism is indicative of religious-cultural and sociopolitical diversity. Language is the experience of religious reality and religion is the form of its expression. He poses the question: What is the fundamental reality which a given culture apprehends by its language and symbols? In response to this question he calls attention not only to the sacred Scriptures like the Vedas, but first of all to the language of the people. It is there that one comes into contact with the fundamental values every religion struggles with.

The framework within which he sees Asiatic religiosity operating has two dimensions: (a) cosmic religion which functions as foundation and (b) a meta-cosmic soteriology which constitutes the main building. By "cosmic religion" he understands what often used to be called "animism." The reference is to the fundamental psychological attitude which the religious man *(homo religiosus)* assumes toward the mystery of life. He refers to cosmic forces like heat, fire, wind, cyclones, earth, earthquakes, oceans, rain, floods, things we both need and are afraid of. The formative components of this religiosity are rite, rituals, and a class of mediators. In Asia this religiosity is practically domesticated and integrated in Hinduism, Buddhism, and Taoism, the three "meta-cosmic religions," as Pieris calls them.

According to Pieris, the establishment of the "biblical religions," like Islam in Indonesia and Roman Catholicism in the Philippines, occurred the more easily because there the cosmic religions were still present in an almost pure form. Where, in his opinion, the marriage between cosmic and meta-cosmic religions had been effected, as in Sri

Lanka, India, and Burma, neither Islam nor Christianity were able to wipe them out.

With reference to Buddhism, he remarks that it is pan-Asiatic and has penetrated nearly all linguistic zones (even for a time the Semitic during the mission of Emperor Ashoka to Syria—third century B.C.). In twenty regions in Asia Buddhism is either the official religion or a culturally influential factor. Hinduism and Taoism, on the other hand, have practically remained limited to one linguistic group. In the third place, Pieris refers to the overwhelming presence of "non-Christian" soteriologies. He considers at length the image of institutional Buddhism with its cosmic and meta-cosmic dimensions of religious experience.[17]

*   *   *

It would be utterly fascinating to consider a larger number of contributions by Christian (and for that matter non-Christian) theologians and thinkers to this Asiatic image of Jesus Christ. Japan comes to mind as one example.

In the difficult years which followed World War II, in which Japan suffered defeat, Kazo Kitamori wrote his theology of "the pain of God." In more recent years the works of Kosuke Koyama have become widely known. Tsutomu Shoji has written with reference to Kitamori that his theology comports well with the painful sense of life characteristic of the Japanese during their long history under the government of the Samurai and military regimes. But, says he, that kind of understanding of the Christian gospel was primarily restricted to the psychological and personal level and did not open the eyes of Christians to the social conditions which meant misery to so many people. Accordingly, the concept of salvation was also restricted to that level.

17. Pieris, "Towards an Asian Theology," pp. 19ff., 29, 35.

Another theologian, Takizawa Katsumi, has therefore stated that the original fact of "Immanuel" requires both a theological and a political "engagement" with contemporary problems.[18]

Furthermore, contributions to Asiatic "Christology" from Korea[19] and Indonesia[20] could be discussed. However, in this book we shall only deal at somewhat greater length with the images of Christ that have arisen in the context of India and China.

18. England, *Living Theology,* pp. 56 and 35 respectively; cf. further K. Kitamori, *Theology of the Pain of God* (Tokyo: John Knox Press, 1958); K. Koyama, *Waterbuffalo Theology* (London: SCM, 1974), *No Handle on the Cross* (Maryknoll, NY: Orbis, 1979), and *Mount Fuji and Mount Sinai: A Pilgrimage in Theology* (London: SCM, 1984); Shusaku Endo, *A Life of Jesus* (Mahwah, NJ: Paulist Press, 1979).

19. Kim Young Bock, ed., *Minjung Theology: People as the Subjects of History* (Singapore: The Commission on Theological Concerns, The Christian Conference of Asia, 1981).

20. Cf. "Jesus as Guru—A Theology in the Context of Java (Indonesia)" *Exchange Bulletin of Third World Christian Literature* 13, 39 (Dec. 1984); P. van Akkeren, *Sri and Christ: A Study of the Indigenous Church in East Java* (London: Lutterworth, 1970); cf. for this subject in general, A. G. Honig, *De kosmische betekenis van Christus in de hedendaagse Aziatische theologie* (Kampen: Kok, 1984); Vinay Samuel and C. Sugden, eds., *Sharing Jesus in the Two Thirds World* (Grand Rapids: Eerdmans, 1984).

V 2. CHRIST OF THE INDIAN ROAD

*T*HE *Christ of the Indian Road* is the title of a fascinating book by the well-known evangelist and missionary E. Stanley Jones. It raises the question: How was and is Jesus understood and in what way does he go down India's roads?

At the third General Assembly of the World Council of Churches in New Delhi in 1961—the first and till now the only one such meeting held in Asia—there was a discussion in the "Witness" section about the necessity of dialogue with other traditions about their changing faiths. "We must take up the conversations about Christ with them, knowing that Christ addresses them through us and us through them."[1] Now as far as India is concerned, a response to Christ was being shaped for a long time already.[2] Stanley Samartha, for instance, makes a distinction between response to Christ without commitment to him, response *and* commitment to Christ outside the context of the institutional church, and response and commitment plus entry into the church.[3]

1. World Council of Churches, Third Assembly, Delhi, 1961, *New Delhi Speaks*, W. A. Visser 't Hooft, ed. (New York: Association Press, 1962), p. 82.
2. M. M. Thomas, *The Acknowledged Christ of the Indian Renaissance* (London: SCM, 1969).
3. S. J. Samartha, *The Hindu Response to the Unbound Christ* (Madras: Christian Literature Society for India, 1974), p. 117.

135

Christ in the posture of a preacher
A depiction of Christ by A. Alphonso. Head, shoulders, and especially the gesturing right hand are reminiscent of the preaching Buddha. The curled form of the hair and nose are taken from the folk art of India. According to the painter, the extra large eyes which have neither pupil nor iris have been represented like this "because spiritual eyes are hard to render."

In the category of those who did respond to Christ but remained Hindu, mention can be made of Raja Rammohan Roy (1772-1833), who worked out a Christology of a moral Christ against the background of Indian theism. One may think also of the "mystical Christ" of Shri Ramakrishna (1836-1886), who received a vision of Christ. He believed that Christ was an incarnation of God but not the only one. Another example of a response without commitment, as Samartha speaks of it—at least in the sense of nonassociation with a church—is Mahatma Gandhi.

GANDHI AND CHRIST

One of Gandhi's favorite songs was: "When I Survey the Wondrous Cross." It is reported that Gandhi was deeply touched by the picture of the crucified Christ wearing only a loincloth, such as poor men in the villages of India wear.[4]

Mahatma Gandhi regarded Jesus as the highest *Satyagrahi* (one devoted to the Truth). " 'The message of Jesus, as I understand it, is contained in his Sermon on the Mount,' " says Gandhi. " 'The Spirit of the Sermon on the Mount competes almost on equal terms with the *Bhagavadgita* for the domination of my heart. It is that Sermon which has endeared Jesus to me.' " "When he read the Sermon on the Mount, especially such passages as 'Resist not evil,' he says, 'I was simply overjoyed and found my own opinion confirmed where I least expected it. The *Bhagavadgita* deepened the impression, and Tolstoy's *The Kingdom of God is Within You* gave it permanent form.' " " 'The gentle figure of Christ, so patient, so kind, so loving, so full of forgiveness that he taught his followers not to retaliate when abused or struck

4. Samartha, p. 92; R. W. Taylor, *Jesus in Indian Paintings* (Madras: Christian Literature Society for India, 1975), p. 63.

but to turn the other cheek—it was a beautiful example, I
thought, of the perfect man.'" He accepted Jesus as "'a
martyr, an embodiment of sacrifice' and the Cross as 'a great
example to the world'. . . 'Though I cannot claim to be a
Christian in the sectarian sense, the example of Jesus' suffering is a factor in the composition of my underlying faith in
non-violence [*ahimsa*], which rules all my actions, worldly
and temporal. Jesus lived and died in vain, if he did not
teach us to regulate the whole of life by the eternal Law of
Love.'"

In all this Gandhi was not interested in a historical
Jesus. "'I should not care if it was proved by someone that
the man called Jesus never lived, and that what was nar-
rated in the Gospels was a figment of the writer's imagination. For the Sermon on the Mount would still be true
to me.' 'To those who live the Sermon, the birth, death, and
continued presence of Christ are not historical but ever-
recurring eternal events in the moral life of every individual or corporate self engaged in sacrificial love.'"
"'As long as it remains a hunger still unsatisfied, as long
as Christ is not yet born, we shall have to look forward to
him. When real peace is established, we will not need
demonstration, but it will be echoed in our life. . . . Then
we will not think of a particular day in the year as that of
the birth of Christ but as an ever-recurring event which
can be enacted in every life. . . . God did not bear the Cross
only nineteen hundred years ago, but He bears it today,
and He dies and is resurrected from day to day.'"

Gandhi rejected the notion of "divine atonement and
forgiveness through Jesus Christ . . . His reason [was he]
was not ready 'to believe literally that Jesus by his death and
by his blood redeemed the sins of the world'" and his heart
refused to accept 'that there was anything like a mysterious
or miraculous virtue in Jesus' death on the Cross.'"

"Similarly, Gandhi found that the idea of divine grace

through Christ offering men freedom from law was a source of moral license." "Any idea of a unique place for the Person or work of Jesus Christ in the moral and spiritual progress of mankind is ruled out. Gandhi is prepared to consider Jesus Christ as one of the many teachers and prophets of mankind, and even as one of the many names and incarnations of God, but without giving his divine nature, his atoning deed or his mediation between God and mankind any uniqueness." " 'God alone is absolutely perfect.' " "Gandhi believes that revelation is not the monopoly of any one nation or tribe." " 'There is only one God but there are many paths to Him.'" " 'The highest truth needs no communicating, for it is by its very nature self-propelling. It radiates its influence silently as the rose its fragrance without the intervention of a medium.' " Gandhi "does not believe in 'people telling others of their faith,' for 'faith does not admit of telling; it has to be lived and then it becomes self-propagating.'"[5]

Gandhi's idea of a universalized Christianity arises, first and foremost, "from his understanding of Christ as the symbol of the eternal law of *ahimsa* (non-violence), expressed in the Sermon on the Mount." In his opinion, therefore, Christianity in its essence is "a new life and not a religion, and wherever the way of love is practiced, Christianity is present. Not Christology but ethics as the means to Truth constitutes fundamental Christianity, and it is the same in all religions."

" 'It is not he who says, Lord, Lord, that is a Christian, but he that does the will of the Lord. . . . And cannot he who has not heard the name of Christ Jesus do the will of the Lord?' " It is Gandhi's conviction that when the church received the backing of a Roman emperor, Christianity changed into an "imperialistic faith." He believes that

5. As summarized by Thomas, pp. 198, 202, 203, 207.

Indian Christians must dissociate themselves from Western civilization which is based on violence and material-
ism.[6]

INDIAN CHRISTIANS AND JESUS CHRIST

This is the time and place to yield the stage to certain Indian
theologians who have to formulate a "Christology" or doctrine of Christ in their own Indian context. How do they
view Jesus in relation to Hinduism and its culture?

A number of years ago two Christological designs
were offered. A. J. Appasamy, at one time a bishop of the
church of South Asia, elaborated especially the Johannine
components in the understanding of Jesus (so typical of
much Indian Christian thought) in order thus to approxi-
mate the Bhakti religion.[7]

V. Chakkarai, author of *Jesus the Avatara*, wanted to
return from Christological speculation to the contemplation
of the life of Jesus itself in order to discover in him what
religious experience and God-consciousness looks like.[8]

Then in the early years of this century there was J. N.
Farquhar, who spoke of Christianity as "The crown of Hinduism."[9]

6. Thomas, pp. 208, 209.

7. A. J. Appasamy, *Christianity as Bhakti Marga; A Study of the Johannine Doctrine of Love* (Madras: Christian Literature Society for India, 1926[2]);
The Gospel and India's Heritage (New York: Macmillan, 1942).

8. V. Chakkarai, *Jesus the Avatara* (Madras: Christian Literature
Society for India, 1930[2]); *The Cross and Indian Thought* (Madras: Christian
Literature Society for India, 1932).

9. J. N. Farquhar, *The Crown of Hinduism* (London: H. Milford, 1913).

THE UNKNOWN CHRIST OF HINDUISM

The Unknown Christ of Hinduism is the title of a book by a Roman Catholic Indian theologian Raimundo Panikkar (b. 1918). He studied the Vedanta as well as the Bible, and became thoroughly at home both in Thomistic and in Vedanta terminology. Vedanta literally means "end of the Vedas," the holy books of the Hindus. The Advaita (nonduality, Shankara's system of Vedanta) is one of the forms of the Vedanta which has its roots in the Upanishads. The teaching of the Upanishads essentially comes down to the position that the essence of the macrocosm and microcosm are identical. The Indian thinker and philosopher Shankara (788-822), in his Advaitic system, drew from this doctrine the conclusion that God, world, and man can be apprehended in a single conception.

Both in his *The Unknown Christ of Hinduism* and in his *Trinity and World Religions*, Panikkar employs a technical terminology derived from Thomistic philosophy as well as from the Vedanta: he seeks to understand Hinduism from the inside out. Especially two Bible texts have significantly influenced Panikkar: "In past generations he allowed all the nations to walk in their own ways; yet he did not leave himself without witness" (Acts 14:16, 17) and "What therefore you worship as unknown, this I proclaim to you" (Acts 17:23). These texts lead him to the conclusion "that Christ is present in Hinduism" and therefore that Hinduism became an effective means for millions of people to bring them salvation and union with God, precisely on account of "the hidden presence of Christ" in it. In Christianity Christ was fully revealed. The work of Christian missions is therefore to disclose "the hidden Christ of Hinduism." He refers to the idea of Christianity as Hinduism that died and rose again as now "transformed." His thesis is that when Indians think of Ishvara—the "true revealer of Brahman" (the Ulti-

Indonesian Crucifix
This depiction of the crucifix is by the Indonesian artist Bagong Kussudiardja, considered a master of the traditional art of batik painting.

mate Reality), "agent of creation, origin of grace"—they in fact, without knowing it, acknowledge "the hidden Christ" (the unknown trinity of the great faiths).[10]

Accordingly, Panikkar comes to the conclusion that Christ is already present in Hinduism, although he is not recognized as Christ. "Christ has not unveiled his whole face, has not yet completed his mission there. He still has to grow up and to be recognized. Moreover, he still has to be crucified there, dying with Hinduism as he died with Judaism and with the Hellenistic religions in order to rise again, as the same Christ (who is already in Hinduism), but then as a risen Hinduism, as Christianity.[11]

THE UNBOUND CHRIST

Stanley Samartha's Christological design of "the unbound Christ" was also formulated in association with Vedanta philosophy. In his work one encounters on the one hand a plea for openness toward Advaitic thought and, on the other, a critique of it. His concern is certainly not to offer a simple adaptation.

His criticism of Advaita philosophy, a running theme throughout his work, can be summarized in two essential points:

1. The search for the ground of existence culminating in the *Brahman* results in the minimalization of the meaning of world history.

2. The search for the essential nature of man culminating in the *atman* results in a devaluation of human personal-

10. R. Boyd, *An Introduction to Indian Christian Theology* (reprint, Madras: Christian Literature Society for India, 1979), pp. 222-23.

11. R. Panikkar, *The Unknown Christ of Hinduism* (London: Darton, Longman & Todd, 1964), p. 17, 1981²; cf. *The Trinity and World Religions* (Madras, 1970).

ity. This double search, in his opinion, determined the viewpoint of the classic *advaita,* which shows a tendency to
neglect the social dimension of human life.[12]

Samartha believes that in the Indian *karma-samsāra*—
that is, the doctrine that teaches that man's place in the chain
of births and rebirths depends on the sum of his
(mis)deeds—the freedom and responsibility of the individual personality do not get enough attention. He
believes, further, that the social and historical dimensions of
human life are shortchanged. There is in this mode of
thought, in his view, no possibility for the emergence of the
new either in nature or in history. Further, the reality of
tragedy and evil within human spirituality sometimes
masquerading as goodness is neglected. There is, in this
scheme, no awareness of the persistence of sin, guilt, and
death in human existence (e.g., the arms race with its potential for total destruction), nor of the possibility of an abrupt
finis to human existence without its ever having had an
opportunity of reaching its *telos.*[13]

One is struck by the frequency with which Samartha
cites the basis-formula of the World Council of Churches
("Jesus Christ as Lord and Saviour") as the point of departure for his Christology. The motivation for his study "is the
search for a genuine Christology in India, a Christology
which, while being rooted in the heritage of the country,
would at the same time be meaningful to the personal and
social needs of the day."[14]

Samartha, who is critical of specifically Indian
thought, is also unsparing in his criticism of Western theology. He is especially opposed to the type of Christian
theology or thought, which views God's revelation as re-

12. Samartha, p. 171.
13. Samartha, pp. 192, 193.
14. Samartha, p. 116.

stricted to the historical. In this way, he says, revelation is dissociated from nature on the one hand, and from human consciousness on the other. The Hindu view, which thinks in terms of the unity of all life, can offer a correction at this point. "This is not to deny the distinctiveness of the biblical faith but only to point out that while emphasising history as the category of God's revelation the unity of life that embraces nature, history, and consciousness should not be ignored."[15]

It is Samartha's intent to unite Christian ideas with Hindu thought in such a way that somehow justice is done to both. He asks himself whether that is possible. After all, so often people have the idea that in Indian thought the Brahman would never allow for union with the personal and that the world is regarded as unreal or *maya* (illusion).

Samartha takes a firm stand against such general statements as though "Hindus believe in the impersonal Brahman, whereas the Christians believe in a personal God."

According to him, "Brahman, properly interpreted, need not be incompatible with personal values." And in his opinion "the description of the world as 'maya' does not indicate its status."[16] *Maya* is not pure illusion, but must rather be viewed as a description of the relation of the world to God. It emphasizes that only Brahman is real. Brahman is *advitiya*, one "without a second"—all else must be viewed as *maya* "in the sense of having no absolute reality but only a dependent and derived status." Shankara's *Mayavada* does not, says Samartha, deny the reality of this world. The phenomenal world is real, although it does not have the same reality as God. It is not nothing; rather, because God wills it to be, it is real.[17]

15. Samartha, p. 177.
16. Samartha, p. 177.
17. Samartha, pp. 181, 182.

Hence it is not impossible, according to Samartha, to "relate Jesus to the *Brahman* on the one hand and with the world on the other, thus bringing the dimensions of the personal and the historical within the structure of Hindu spirituality."[18]

The New Testament witnesses to the Christ event and its implications for "personal, historical and social life. But there is also an effort made to go beyond the historical into the cosmic. The confession of Christ as the agent in creation so strongly articulated in the Fourth Gospel, Colossians, and Hebrews . . . is perhaps one of the most crucial points where Christology can make a genuine contribution in the context of *advaita* as it grapples with the meaning of the cosmos that includes nature and history in the totality of its scheme."[19]

When John the Baptist asks Jesus, "Are you he who is to come, or shall we look for another?" (Luke 7:20; Matt. 11:3), Jesus, without answering directly, "points to a concrete set of facts: Look around and see for yourselves what is happening." "What is demanded of us is to open our eyes and ears" to him "who is constantly 'the Coming One.'" The pivotal question is, "*Who* is he in whose name there is

---

18. Samartha, p. 177; cf. also P. Devanandan, *The Concept of Maya* (London: Lutterworth, 1950). Whereas Shankara denies all reality to the world, saying it is *maya* because only Brahman is real, Ramanuja grants a certain reality to the world, saying it is related to God as body to the soul. Appasamy, whom we have mentioned before, has given a Christian explanation of this. In a Christological context he writes: "Thus God took, as it were, a second body, the fleshly organism of Jesus. . . . God revealed himself to men through the human body of Jesus." A. J. Appasamy, *The Gospel and India's Heritage*, p. 207. Appasamy here uses Ramanuja's analogy to show that Christ is a single personality, a unity of body and soul, with a complete created body, in which God nevertheless lives as an internal controller or *antaryamin;* R. H. S. Boyd, *India and the Latin Captivity of the Church: The Cultural Context of the Gospel* (New York: Cambridge Univ. Press, 1974), p. 28.

19. Samartha, p. 183.

salvation, healing and renewal?" In this connection Samartha wants to stress that the name Christ, biblically and theologically, cannot be restricted to the historical figure of Jesus of Nazareth. "He who was before Abraham (John 8:58), he who is the same yesterday, today and tomorrow (Heb. 13:8), he who is the Logos and who became flesh (John 1:14), is also the One who is continuing his work today."

"If we take seriously the implications of our faith, viz., that we believe in the *living* God, in Christ who is the Lord of *history*, including contemporary history, and in the promise that the Spirit will guide us into all truth, then can we deny that Christ is at work wherever people are struggling for freedom and renewal, seeking for fulness of life, peace and joy"?[20]

Klaus Klostermaier has remarked that India's great concern is *Brahmavidya:* the knowledge of the highest union with the absolute. Christ is the revelation of God and he leads us to the deepest and highest levels of *Brahmavidya.* Greek Christology, he says, has not exhausted the mystery of Christ though it has helped the church to see certain aspects of Christ more clearly. Indian wisdom will not exhaust the mystery of Christ either. But it will help the church of India to understand Christ better and to make him really understood—knowing Christ as the revelation of the mystery of *Brahmavidya:* Christ, the fervent longing of the everlasting hills.[21]

20. Samartha, "Mission and Movements of Innovation," in *Mission Trends No. 3*, G. H. Anderson and T. F. Stransky, eds. (Grand Rapids: Eerdmans, 1976), pp. 242, 243.

21. K. Klostermaier, *Christ und Hindu in Vrindaban* (Cologne: Hegner, 1968), pp. 155-56; cf. Boyd, *Indian Christian Theology,* p. 86.

V 3. CHRIST AND TAO

JUNG Young Lee, a Korean theologian, in designing a Christology which takes Taoism into its purview, links Jesus
Christ with this world of thought and life, one that is so
characteristic for the Chinese world. His premise is that the
either/or way of thinking—with its tendency to absolutize
and exclude a middle way of both/and—is "responsible for
the predicament of Christianity in the world today."

Over against this Western tendency he proposes the
Chinese concept of change and relativity, expressed in the
interplay of *yin* and *yang,* which he says "provides a much
needed category of thinking that can be helpful 'not only for
the development of ecumenical theology but for the mutual
co-existence of Christianity with other religions in a creative
process of becoming.' He maintains that *yin-yang* thinking—'a way of both/and thinking which includes the possibility of either/or'—will not only 'solve controversial issues in theology but . . . bring to light new meaning and
fresh understanding of theological issues.' "[1]

1. Jung Young Lee, "The Yin-Yang Way of Thinking: A Possible
Method for Ecumenical Theology," in *Mission Trends No. 3,* G. H. Ander-
son and T. F. Stransky, eds. (Grand Rapids: Eerdmans, 1976), p. 29; *The I:
A Christian Concept of Man* (New York: Philosophical Library, 1971); *The
Principle of Changes: Understanding the I Ching* (New York: New Hyde Park
University Books, 1971).

In his *The Theology of Change: A Christian Concept of God in an Eastern Perspective,*[2] Lee speaks of Christ as "the perfect realization of change." In Lee's opinion, "Christian theology has paid more attention to Christ and his work than to God as creator and has commonly regarded the event of salvation as distinct from, and more important than, the event of creation." Thus "the continuity between God's creative work and his saving work has in the past been largely ignored, the saving work being attributed exclusively to the Christ and the creative work to the Father" (p. 86).

But "God the savior and God the creator are one and inseparable.". . . "Salvation is presupposed in creation, but creation is absolutely necessary to salvation because salvation means a return to the original creation . . . Jesus Christ said again and again that he came to the world to fulfill the will of his Father, the creator." . . . "If Christ came to do his Father's work, then what Christ did, the work of salvation, was the creator's work" (p. 87).

God as Creator "is the source of creativity and the source of all that is and will be, while Christ is only what is manifested of God." When the Creator is identified with the Redeemer Christ, the "inexhaustible nature of the divine creativity" is denied. "God as creator is more than what is manifested and his mystery is not and will not be exhausted." 'This non-identity of God and the Son is based upon the fact that God alone is Creator but that the Son is called simply and solely the mediator of the Creation' (Emil Brunner). "In other words, Christ is subordinate to the creator and his work as savior and redeemer is one part of the work of God as creator" (p. 88).

---

2. Jung Young Lee, *The Theology of Change: A Christian Concept of God in an Eastern Perspective* (Maryknoll, NY: Orbis, 1979). (All further references are made parenthetically.)

CHRIST AS THE WORD

"Christ as the foundation of the creative process is clearly expressed in the story of creation, where Christ is identical with the Word coming from the mouth of the Creator." The creation story, says Lee, "may be the best place to begin the study of Christology because 'the Word' is more expressive of Christ than any other name." "To the Hebraic mind, Christ as the Word of God was . . . the dynamic force that changes and produces new life and new possibilities. The Word, which in Greek thought is analogous to Reason, is in the Hebrew mind almost identical with the Deed of God."

"Genesis narrates the creation in detail in order to emphasize that God is the creator. The Fourth Gospel summarizes the process of creation for the purpose of emphasizing that Christ is the Word, . . . the basis of God's creativity" (pp. 89-90).

CHRIST AS THE LIGHT

"Christ as the Word or the core of creative process is the solution to the existential problem, the problem of estrangement or sin. Christ as the Word is God in existence, as differentiated from God in essence. Since Christ is God in existence, that is, God in manifestation, he is conditionally limited."

"Christ as light cannot be excluded from the darkness, because light cannot exist without darkness nor darkness without light. . . . Because Christ subjected himself to the condition of existence, the darkness must also be in his light. Conversely, Christ as light enters into our darkness. The relationship between Christ as light and life and the world as darkness and death can be illustrated by the *Tai chi t'u*, the diagram of the Great Ultimate in the *I ching*. This dia-

Jesus teaching in the temple
In this depiction by the Chinese painter Ch'en, Jesus is represented as a little Chinese philosopher amidst Chinese wise men.

gram consists of interlocked but differentiated *yin* (darkness) and *yang* (light)."

"It is important to notice, however, that the *yin* portion of the diagram contains a *yang,* or light, dot, and the *yang* portion contains a *yin* dot. Christ as light, or *yang,* is not entirely exclusive of *yin* or darkness, and the world as *yin* or darkness is not entirely exclusive of *yang* or light. The expansion of light *(yang)* in darkness *(yin)* is a metaphor of the process of redemption or the growth of Christ-consciousness in us. Redemption, which is Christ, grows within us just as we grow within Christ's redemptive work, which is part of his creative work" (pp. 91-92; cf. 38-40).

CHRIST AS THE SAVIOR

"The idea of existential estrangement resembles the Buddhist idea of *dukkha. Dukkha* is usually translated as 'suffering' but the word is better translated 'existential estrangement.' The Pali word *dukkha* refers literally to an axle that is off-center with respect to its wheel or to a bone that has slipped out of its socket. Therefore *dukkha* implies an existential estrangement, an estrangement of relationship. Since life is in a state of *dukkha,* or distorted relationship, it is in constant motion and process, it expresses itself as pain and suffering . . . That is why the life of sin is a life of suffering. Moreover, this existential estrangement disrupts the natural process of creativity in the world."

Lee then describes sin as "nothing but humanity's desire to *be* rather than to *become;* it is our unwillingness to change" (see the title of his book). "The desire to be—to remain unchanged in the moving stream of life—is the existential estrangement, or sin. To overcome this desire to be . . . is the goal or salvation, and the restoration of normal creativity."

"Salvation, then, means to follow the way of change without nostalgia. When Jesus said 'I am the Way,' he was referring to the way of change." "He is *yang* and we are *yin*. It is *yang's* function to act and to initiate and *yin's* to respond and follow. Christ is creative because of *yang;* we must be receptive because of *yin*. Our only proper action, as *yin*, is to respond. By our response, however, we become creative, because *yin* becomes *yang* by response and *yang* becomes *yin* by creation. Thus we become active by our inaction, creative by our response, and joyful by our suffering. It is a paradox of Christian experience" (pp. 92-94; cf. 2 Cor. 6:8-10).

"This idea is also expressed in the *Tao te ching*, the Taoist Scripture, which says, 'The Way is gained by daily loss, loss upon loss, until at last comes rest. By letting go, it all gets done; the world is won by those who let it go!'. . . The way of *yin* is to gain by losing itself, or, in Paul's words, 'It is no longer I who live, but Christ who lives in me (Gal. 2:20).' By responding to Christ's call to follow him, we cause him to act in us, as *yang* acts in *yin*. That is how 'by letting go, it all gets done.' The change changes us. . . .By letting go, our way becomes his way and his way becomes ours. That is the secret of the way of change, the *tao*. Christ triumphed by loss of self. By enduring total defeat in crucifixion, he gained complete victory in resurrection. To give in full is to receive in full. . . . Lao Tzu says: 'The movement of the way is a return; in weakness lies its strength.' And Jesus' teaching that the last shall be first and the exalted shall be humbled is identical in meaning." "By letting go of our *being*—of what we *are* at some finite moment—we become one with the way of change and transformation and that is the way of salvation. To be saved means to be part of the process of change and transformation brought about by the power of the change. Salvation is the harmony between the change and the changing or between the creator and the creature. It is like the harmony of *yin* and *yang*" (pp. 94-95).

"Divine creativity, which is perfectly manifested in Christ, is the power of renewal through the constant interplay of *yin* and *yang*. In the Book of Changes [the *I Ching*] there are sixty-four archetypes that are continually renewed to create new existences. They are essentially unchanging, even though they are manifest as many different forms in existence. Thus the change does not create anything really new but renews the old.... As *yin* grows, *yang* decays; as *yang* grows, *yin* decays.... In fact, salvation history includes both progression and retrogression. The end of time, or *eschaton* must not be understood as the ultimate termination of history. *Eschaton* is the end of the old as well as the beginning of the new, that is, the renewal of the old" (pp. 95-96).

CHRIST AS THE CENTER OF THE CREATIVE PROCESS

"Christ as the center of the cosmic process is analogous to the Indian symbol of ... Brahman." "The cosmic Christ also represents the center of the human soul and the axis of human life." "In the center of the changing process, which is Christ, not only all things but all times—past, present, and future—come together.... Therefore to be in the center of changing process is also to be in eternity. By saying 'I am the Alpha and Omega, the first and the last, the beginning and the end' (Rev. 22:13), Jesus meant that he is eternal. In the primordial center he is one 'who is and who was and who is to come' (Rev. 1:8). He is then the symbol of eternal change, which is the perfect manifestation of change itself. . . . Because Christ occupies the center of creative process, where *maya* and sin do not exist, salvation is in him" (pp. 97-98).

THE DIVINITY AND HUMANITY OF CHRIST

"As the primordial origin of the creative process, Christ is
also both divine and human. In this center the distinction
between man and God disappears. . . . Christ as the
primordial center of the creative process is the perfect incarnation of the infinite in the finite world; he is human and
divine in the fullest sense. . . . As a true brother he shows us
the way to the Father, and as a true friend he lays down his
life for us. He is a man for others, standing in the place where
others must stand but cannot."

"The relationship between Christ's divinity and
humanity is like the relationship between *yin* and *yang*. Just
as *yang* cannot exist without *yin* nor *yin* without *yang,* the
humanity of Jesus cannot exist without the divinity of Christ
nor the divinity of Christ without the humanity of Jesus."
Himself "the symbol of perfect harmony between the
change and the changing, Jesus Christ is the ultimate reality
of change and transformation" (pp. 98-99).

THE CRUCIFIXION AND RESURRECTION OF CHRIST

"Christ's resurrection is not the conquest of death but the
fulfillment of life, and his crucifixion was necessary for that
fulfillment. What is to be renewed must first die. Thus Jesus
as the perfect symbol of the change unites both decay and
growth or death and resurrection in the process of constant
change and transformation. . . . Crucifixion and resurrection are *yin* and *yang,* the gateways to all changes, and they
occur in all things, because all things change. If crucifixion
and resurrection are common to all things, how are Jesus'
crucifixion and resurrection unique?" Jesus' cross and resurrection are unique, "not because they happened to him,

but because they became the primordial symbol of all changing" (pp. 100-101).

YIN AND *YANG*

"The concept of *yin* originally came from the imagery of shadow, while that of *yang* from brightness. *Yin* then came to signify female, receptive, passive, cold, etc., and *yang* male, creative, active, warm, etc." Thus in a final analysis "everything, whether spiritual or material and temporal or spatial, can be categorized by the symbol of the interplay between *yin* and *yang*. The symbol of *yin* and *yang* is then the primordial category of everything that exists in the world. The characteristic nature of this symbol is not the conflict but the complementarity of opposites. It is the category of wholeness rather than of partiality. It is the category of becoming rather than of being."

"*Yin* presupposes the necessity of *yang* and *yang* cannot exist without *yin*." "The both/and category of thinking, which is based on the *yin-yang* symbolism, is characteristic not only of the Chinese but also of the Indian way of thinking."[3]

It is Lee's conviction that such concepts as the nature of divine transcendence and immanence, God as personal, Jesus as the Christ, or the relation of body and spirit can all be illuminated by the *yin-yang* mode of thinking. "Jesus as the Christ, as both God and man, cannot really be understood in terms of either/or. How can man also be God? In the West we have to speak in terms of paradox or mystery in order to justify the reality of Christ. However, in *yin-yang* terms, he can be thought of as both God and man at the same

3. Lee, "The Yin-Yang Way," pp. 34-35.

time. In him God is not separated from man nor man from God. They are in complementary relationship. He is God because of man: he is man because of God."[4]

In this chapter we dealt briefly with only a few of the Asiatic features of the face of Jesus. The images of Jesus in India alone are more numerous than we could mention. Especially the relation between Jesus Christ and Buddha deserves further reflection.[5] But perhaps enough has been said to convey an impression of the different ways of understanding Jesus present in the eminently pluralistic context of Asia.

4. Lee, "The Yin-Yang Way," p. 37.
5. For this subject, cf. the articles of A. Pieris referred to in chapter V, part 1, and J. Cobb, *Christ in a Pluralistic Age* (Philadelphia: Westminster, 1974), p. 20; R. H. Drummond, *Gautama the Buddha: An Essay in Religious Understanding* (Grand Rapids: Eerdmans, 1974); H. de Lubac, *La rencontre de Bouddhisme et de l'occident* (Paris: Aubier Éditions Montaigne, 1952).

VI WHO DO YOU SAY THAT I AM?

That you, being rooted and grounded in love, may have power to comprehend with all the saints what is the breadth and length and height and depth, and to know the love of Christ which surpasses knowledge, that you may be filled with all the fulness of God.

Ephesians 3:17-19

So far we have been introduced to various images of Jesus. The focus in each section was the question how Jesus was handed down, received, and perceived in different cultures. We obviously had to be selective; we could not possibly cover everything.

Numerous fundamental questions raised in preceding chapters deserve an answer. Both Jewish and Islamic voices focused on the question whether Christians do not often speak of Jesus in a way which equates him with God. The Koran's objection to the Christian interpretation of the person and work of Jesus has to do especially with this point. These "counter-voices" suggest that Christians of whatever cultural background not speak about Jesus in a way which seems to threaten belief in *one* God.

On the basis of the New Testament witness there can be no doubt that the faith of the historical Jesus had God himself at its center. In Mark (12:29, 30) Jesus cites as the first commandment the well-known confession of Deuteronomy 6:4: "Hear, O Israel: the Lord our God is one Lord." In conversation with the rich young ruler, when the latter calls him "Good Teacher," Jesus answers: "Why do you call me good? No one is good but God alone" (Mark 10:18; cf. Luke 18:19).

Although the portrayal of Jesus given by Naguib Maḥfūz may not be representative of the Islamic view in general, it still provides an exceptional insight into the meaning of Jesus' life, suffering, and death. It is a genuine challenge for a Christian to see here how a Muslim pictures Jesus' way of nonviolence, his nonattachment to power and possessions, and his utterly "spiritual" type of ministry (Jesus as exorcist), action experienced by those in power as a threat. In the end it is the reason why they have him executed.

When a black theologian like Gayraud Wilmore points out how in time Jesus became "white" when Christians came into contact with other races, one can indeed remark that the original renderings of Jesus did not intend to depict a "Semite." But it is correct that, as Western missions passed on their portrayal of Christ, this "trans-coloration" of Jesus (as a European and white man) did occur—at the expense of the real "transmission."

Still, we cannot possibly discuss all the facets of the images of Jesus portrayed in various cultures, nor answer all the questions they evoke. Over and over, as we aimed at a contextual understanding of Jesus Christ, the question which stared us in the face was: What is authentic, and what is false, contextualization? Where was Jesus Christ portrayed and where was he betrayed?

The crucial questions we do want to raise and to which we do want to respond in this final chapter are these:

A. What is the relation of Jesus Christ to the various cultures of the world?
B. What is the relation between these images of Jesus and the New Testament?
C. Is Jesus Redeemer and/or Liberator?
D. Finally, what is the relation between knowing Jesus Christ and following him?

A. CHRIST AND "THE CULTURES"

In our time the question of the relation of Jesus Christ and of Christianity to culture is again forcing itself upon us. At the meeting of the Commission for World Mission and Evangelism in Bangkok in 1973–74 it was said that culture constitutes the human voice which responds to the voice of Christ.

Choan-Seng Song, an Asiatic theologian, has said that Christians "who are not endowed with German eyes should not be prevented from seeing Christ differently. They must train themselves to see Christ through Chinese eyes, Japanese eyes, African eyes, Latin American eyes."[1]

He himself then offers as an example the *Cross of Christ* by the Japanese Christian artist, Giichro Hayakawa. "The whole picture is a paragon of tranquillity in the midst of a raging storm." He calls it a *sibui*-Christ. *Sibui* is a quality which "conveys a controlled reserve toward life and the world." *Sibui* is "eloquent in silence, aggressive in reservation, forceful in reserve." "It is a *sibui* Christ that we encounter here, a Christ who does not show internal emotion and passion, a Christ who faces death and equanimity. Is this not a *sibui* spirituality that is seen in the Savior of the world?"[2]

1. Choan-Seng Song, *Third-Eye Theology: Theology in Formation in Asian Settings* (Maryknoll, NY: Orbis, 1979), p. 11.
2. Song, pp. 9, 12.

The question which arises is whether all those "other" images we have looked at are correct and true-to-life, parts of the whole together forming the complete portrayal of Jesus Christ. Or was there something else going on— betrayal, denial, obfuscation of the image of Jesus? Is no view of Christ, no picture of him, free from falsification, as Song asserts?[3]

Several decades ago H. Richard Niebuhr, in his book *Christ and Culture,* distinguished five positions which can be used with regard to this question; perhaps they can serve our search for an answer to the question concerning the relation of Christ to a variety of different cultures. He mentions these positions: (1) Christ against culture, (2) Christ of culture, (3) Christ above culture, (4) Christ and culture in paradox, and (5) Christ the transformer of culture.

The unsatisfactory feature of the first, says Niebuhr, is that it leads to the kind of spiritualism which abandons the world to its fate. Nor is he happy with the second, as it comes to expression, for example, in cultural Protestantism. In this scheme Christ becomes the fulfiller of the highest expectations of a given culture. Niebuhr's preference obviously lies in the last three positions because, while on the one hand they bring culture under judgment, they nevertheless find a way to confirm it. As the most important representative of the "Christ-above-culture" position, he mentions Thomas Aquinas. Aquinas taught that though people can attain a partial fulfillment of their own, the achievement of ultimate humanity can only occur as a result of divine grace. One of the objections Niebuhr advances against this position is that such acceptance of society produces a religion which is culturally, socially, and politically conservative.

The fourth position, "Christ and culture in paradoxical

3. Song, p. 12.

relation," though it does distinguish between Christ and culture, nevertheless clings to both. Adherents of this pattern are impressed by God's forgiveness and atonement and hence also by human sinfulness. Martin Luther, according to Niebuhr, fits this pattern.

From the design of Niebuhr's book it is clear that he is working toward the fifth as the most reasonable position. Basic to the viewpoint that "Christ transforms culture" are three theological convictions.

1. Humanity lives by the power of the word of creation and for that reason God's creative goodness can be found in human culture.
2. People turn the goodness inherent in creation around by their perverse rebellion against God. The culture may be sinful, but no apocalyptic revision is demanded—no new creation—only a radical conversion.
3. History becomes an open, dynamic interaction between humanity and God.[4]

Applying this scheme to Christ and the different cultures one can say, first of all, that there have always been many who believe that Christ is in (diametrical) opposition to other cultures.

In Asia, as well as in Africa and no less in Latin America (when it concerns indigenous Indian culture and religion), the posture of Christian missions was very often one of "Christ against culture." In Africa the missionaries as a rule were hostile toward traditional religion and culture. African lifestyle was usually completely rejected.[5] The situation in Asia was generally no different.

4. H. Richard Niebuhr, *Christ and Culture* (New York: Harper & Row, 1951), pp. 76ff., 102-8, 148, 152, 159, 191ff.
5. Louisa Ngo Tappa, *Christian Mission and African Culture*, pp. 31, 33.

In defense of a more appreciative attitude toward culture, a statement of Pope Paul VI is sometimes cited, a statement made when in July 1969 he addressed a meeting of African bishops in Kampala, Uganda. On that occasion he said the "language," the manner in which the unique faith of the church is manifested, can take on many forms and hence be original, in keeping with the language, style, temperament, genius, and culture which confesses this unique faith. "In this sense you can and must have African Christianity." As a rule, however, the sentence preceding this quotation, which must at least be said to temper somewhat this openness toward African culture, is not cited: "Above all, your church must be Catholic; in other words, it must be totally founded upon the patrimony, identically, essentially, constitutionally the same teaching as that of Christ, confessed by the authentic tradition, and authorized by the one true church."[6]

One could call Indian Catholic theologians, like J. N. Farquhar and Panikkar,[7] adherents of the third position, "Christ above culture," even with the danger of social and political conservatism which Niebuhr considered inherent in this position. Stanley Samartha's approach fits in best with the fifth position, "Christ the transformer of culture," because he both wants to take the Hindu context thoroughly into account and at the same time is explicitly critical of it.

However illuminating and useful Niebuhr's scheme may be, it still contains a tendency to assume that the identity of Christ is already known. The question which can be put to those who favor the fifth position is this: Who transforms whom? Is it not necessary to say that one must speak of interplay between Christ and the cultures? Not

6. Cited by Tossou K. Raphael Icao, "Théologie africaine: désengagement ou engagement? L'Heure d'un Bilan," *Bulletin Secretariatos Pro-Non-Christianis* 17, 1 (1982): 168, 169.

7. Cf. chapter V, part 2.

only does Christ change and transform (the other) cultures, but it is also true that other cultures and religions bring out features in the face of Christ which had not been revealed before. And therefore must we not add that aspects of Jesus are discovered which *could* not have been known before? It is not only Christ who transforms the *nganga* (medicine man), but it is also the *nganga* who transforms Christ (J. M. Schoffeleers).

Various third-world theologians try to give expression to what in their eyes is the meaning of those other cultures and religions for the understanding of Jesus Christ. According to black theologian Gayraud Wilmore, black theology is discovering the traces of God's presence in the primitive, non-Christian traditions of the past (and which, if this is true, can no longer simply be called non-Christian, one might add). One could refer to Genesis 19, where three men (God) visit Abraham, and to Matthew 25, where Jesus says he is present in the hungry, the thirsty, the stranger, the naked, the sick, and the imprisoned.[8] The African C. B. Okolo says: "The Christian confession of Christ becomes . . . a living and dynamic reality, an existential engagement between Christ and the local culture, the power of the former transforming the latter. . . . Christian culture is therefore one where Christ is not a stranger, where the Christian communities see Christ through the avenues and resources of their own cultures, in their own signs, symbols, and mental categories. . . . For Christianity to be rooted in African soil means to see Christ as African. . . . That does not mean the historical Jesus was an African, but that the Christ of faith can be seen authentically by an African only through his culture and thinking categories, since the leap of faith, like grace, does not destroy but fulfill nature. To see Christ

---

8. G. S. Wilmore and J. H. Cone, *Black Theology, A Documentary History, 1966-1979* (Maryknoll, NY: Orbis, 1979), p. 605.

as African is, in short, to see in Christ an African "Emmanuel," one who dwells among Africans, in their world of meanings, of signs, and symbols."[9]

The idea that such a contextual understanding of Christ, such deep involvement in a specific cultural or other religious context, would and must always automatically lead to syncretism does not stand up in the light of the facts. As an example, one could mention Charles de Foucauld, who, precisely as a result of his penetration of the Islamic world in the Near East and North Africa, (re)discovered his Christian faith.[10] The Indian Manihal C. Parekh (1885-1967), under the influence of the theology of Rammohan Roy, Keshub Chunder Sen, and P. C. Mozoomdar, made the breakthrough into the reality of redemption in Jesus Christ.[11]

Raja Rammohan Roy tells us that through his study of Vaishnavism, the school of Hinduism which believes in incarnation, he began to see the truth of the perfect incarnation of God in Jesus. While the equality of both Hindu and Christian faiths fascinated and attracted him, it was the inequality between the highest incarnations of each which made him choose Christianity over Vashnavism.[12]

The black experience, says James Cone, "is a source of truth but not the truth itself."[13] Accordingly, the "text" and the "context" are not put on the same level; hence there is no preaching of "the Christ of culture," nor of black culture either.

Very often the relation between Jesus Christ or the

9. C. B. Okolo, "'Christ, Emmanuel': An African Inquiry" *Bulletin de theologie africaine* 2 (Jan./July 1980): 16-17.

10. K. Cragg, *Alive to God* (London: Oxford Univ. Press, 1974), intro.

11. M. M. Thomas, *The Acknowledged Christ of the Indian Renaissance* (London: SCM, 1969), p. 12.

12. Thomas, p. 30.

13. J. H. Cone, *God of the Oppressed* (New York: Seabury, 1975), p. 33.

Christian faith and other cultures and religions is viewed as one of fulfillment: the Christian faith or church must somehow "baptize" that other culture or religion.

For Aloysius Pieris this train of thought is an occasion for reflecting on John's baptism of Jesus and its meaning for our missionary method.

John the Baptist, according to Pieris, stood in the ancient deuteronomic tradition of prophetic asceticism in which Jesus found his authentic spirituality, as well as an appropriate starting point for his mission. The people whom John baptized were the religious poor of the land, the stigmatized, the repentant sinners. By having himself baptized by John the Baptist, Jesus identified himself with those religious poor.

Jesus' first gesture—his baptism by John—brought him to an authentic discovery of his task. Pieris expresses the wish that the local church in Asia would be as humble as her bridegroom and Lord. "Would that Christians asked to be baptized rather than to baptize!" By that he means that the Christian faith must not be so anxious to baptize that other culture, its predecessor, but like Jesus should seek to be baptized by it! His wish is that Christianity "would immerse itself in the baptismal water of Asiatic religions which precede Christianity." "It is only in the Jordan of Asiatic religiosity that we shall be recognized as a voice that is worthy to be heard by all! Hear him!"

Pieris calls the church to sit down, like her own teacher, at the feet of Asiatic gurus, not as *ecclesia docens* (teaching church), but as *ecclesia discens* (learning church), lost among the religious poor of Asia, the *anawim* (the devout poor), as the Bible calls them.

Asks Pieris: "Was it not by losing himself among humble but repentant sinners and the religious poor of the land that Jesus . . . discovered his authentic uniqueness as the Lamb of God that delivers us from sin, the beloved Son who may be heard and listened to, the messiah who has a new message and a new baptism to offer?"

This does not mean for Pieris that Jesus has not brought or will not bring something new, or that he would say and do the same as John the Baptist. Jesus was baptized by John, and precisely as such and in that manner he arose to a *new* life, with a *new* mandate, and with *new* insight into his mission. The "newness" of Jesus' message comes out the more conspicuously on account of and through that immersion in the water of the Jordan.

According to Pieris, the spirituality of John the Baptist was traditional and negative; that of Jesus positive and utterly *new*. John cursed religious and political leaders who tried to justify themselves; Jesus blessed marginalized and stigmatized sinners. The Baptist announced the judgment to come, but Jesus whom he baptized offered the good news of the deliverance that was at hand. The beloved Son would rather take upon himself death on the cross for the conversion of the world. John demanded individual conversion; Jesus sought to convert people in the fellowship of love. He immersed himself in the stream of ancient spirituality but emerged with a new mission. Only this baptism offers the Christian identity and the Christian renewal for which we are looking.

Jesus' baptism by John, where he kneels before his predecessor (Mark 1:9-11), and Jesus' cross (Mark 10:45; Luke 12:50), where he as Suffering Servant ends his earthly mission in apparent failure—these are the most self-denying deeds anyone could perform.

Thus Pieris applies the fact that Jesus was the baptized rather than the baptizer, to the attitude the church should adopt. To regain her lost authority the Asiatic church should give up all its links with power. She must be humble enough to have herself baptized in the Jordan of Asiatic religiosity and brave enough to be baptized on the cross of Asiatic poverty. Is it not her fear of losing her identity, he asks, which makes her lean on mammon? Is it not her refusal to die which keeps her from living?[14]

It is Pieris's intent to show that in the matter of the contextual understanding of Jesus Christ we are dealing with two closely related aspects. On the one hand there is the cultural-religious (other than "Christian") aspect, and on the other the sociopolitical. With regard to the first, the issue is "inculturation"—the question of how Jesus is linked with a given culture and how he enters it; and with regard to the second, the issue is his relation to the social and political realities—in what way he is regarded as liberator. By the reference to Jesus' baptism in the Jordan and on the cross, Pieris seeks to make clear that, by being immersed in that religiosity and poverty, the two big realities of Asia, Jesus rises with a new message and a new mission.

This is not to suggest that all the questions evoked by the different Christ images are thereby answered, whether those which have been designed by Setiloane in the African context, Samartha in the context of Hinduism, or by Lee in the Chinese. In the case of the last, for instance, one may ask whether Jesus has not been too much pressed into a kind of unified system, so that there appears to be no room left for the *scandal* (skandalon) of the cross. His cross seems to fit all too easily in a concept of unity which can bridge all opposites. It would seem that the mystery of Jesus Christ, the injustice and guilt he bore, can thus be explained too simply. But Pieris's meditation on Jesus' baptism in the Jordan and on the cross does have the potential for leading people to a really fresh understanding of Jesus in every other cultural, religious, and political context.

14. Aloysius Pieris, "Mission of the Local Church in Relation to Other Major Religious Traditions," *Sedos Bulletin* 82, 5 (Mar. 1982); 6 (Apr. 1982); 7 (May 1982): 123-25; "Western Christianity and Asian Buddhism: A Theological Reading of Historic Encounters," *Dialogue*, n.s. 7 (1980): 49-50.

B. THE IMAGES OF JESUS AND THE NEW TESTAMENT

In the consideration of various images of Jesus Christ, whether "red" or "black," as "Liberator" and/or "Redeemer," the question arises whether for the purpose of evaluation one cannot and must not go back to the New Testament. After all, does not the New Testament contain the criteria in terms of which the various "understandings" of Jesus must be judged and possibly condemned?

Considered by itself, this last assertion is certainly correct, but it looks much simpler than it actually is. One of the very first things to say is that there is no single, homogeneous image of Jesus in the New Testament. One can speak of a variety of Christologies, such as a *Logos* Christology, or a *Kurios*, a prophets', or a high priest, Christology; a discipleship, Servant-of-the-Lord, or Son of God Christology.

One can derive from the New Testament a variety of Christological formulations which correspond to the interpretations of Christ held by Palestinian Jewish Christians, Jewish Christians of the *diaspora*, and Hellenistic Christians. Hans-Ruedi Weber speaks of different traditions which were developed in Jerusalem, Galilee, West Syria, East Syria, or Rome. Even more important for the present-day contextual understanding of Jesus and its evaluation is the realization that already then, within what we today call the New Testament, specific choices were made from the store of memory concerning Jesus. By pointing out the meaning of remembered words or deeds of Jesus, these interpretations answered concrete questions of the day, within a specific cultural context. In this interpretive activity theological, apologetic, pastoral, and missionary motives came into play, suggests Weber. This implies that in the process of interpretation words were used which had not been spoken by Jesus and events were mentioned which did not happen that way in his lifetime.[15]

In other words, the understanding of Jesus reflected in the writings of the New Testament already shows a kind of interplay or two-way traffic. One can speak of a *factual* side, meaning that which actually happened, and an *attributive* side, meaning that which was attributed to Jesus. For example, when Jesus is called "messiah," that term, on the one hand, derives from a certain tradition which exerted a formative influence upon the way Jesus was seen and understood; but on the other hand, and that is the new and "giving" side, so to speak, there is Jesus, the one who gives content and a new structure to the concept of messiah. Accordingly, the various understandings of the truth and meaning of Jesus Christ already present in the New Testament are also dependent on the patterns of pre-Christian understanding operative in the witnesses who saw and heard![16]

If this is true of the witness of the New Testament, is it not also allowable and defensible that the witnesses and hearers in the various other contexts—the African, Asiatic, and Latin American—should help determine what the truth and meaning of Jesus Christ is? The (renewed) understanding of Jesus as exorcist is perhaps a good example of this.

Jesus as Exorcist

A "look" at different images of Jesus can help a person to bring to the fore neglected aspects of Jesus' ministry or to put a new face on them. This is strikingly illustrated in the

15. H. R. Weber, *The Cross: Tradition and Interpretation* (Grand Rapids: Eerdmans, 1975), pp. 85-86.

16. R. H. Fuller, *New Testament Christology* (London, 1965), pp. 243-46; cf. E. Schillebeeckx, *Tussentijds verhaal over twee Jezus boeken* (Bloemendaal: H. Nelissen B.V., 1978).

image of Jesus advanced by a Jew, a Moslem, and an African, in which Jesus' function as exorcist is brought out.

Naguib Maḥfūẓ, in the novel referred to earlier (chap. 2), strongly emphasizes Jesus' role as one who drives out evil spirits. This emphasis recalls certain elements and accents in the gospel stories which, generally speaking, are no longer prominent in "Western" interpretation, but which reappear prominently in a contribution from a Jewish scholar.

Geza Vermes repeatedly speaks of Jesus as exorcist. He relates how Jesus did not practice a secular vocation in the years of his public ministry but devoted himself exclusively to religious activities. The synoptic gospels are unanimous in their representation of Jesus as exorcist, healer, and teacher, with him especially active in Galilee in expelling evil spirits. According to Vermes, Jesus most deeply impressed his contemporaries by his mastery over demons and illness and by the magnetic power of his preaching.

In Jesus' world the devil and evil spirits were believed to be at the root of both sickness and sin, a perspective that took root in Jewish religious thought in the period following the Babylonian exile. Jesus himself defined his ministry in terms of exorcism and healing: his mission was to the sick, the physically and spiritually ill. He was preeminently the healer. Did he not say when sending out the disciples: "Heal the sick, raise the dead, cleanse lepers, cast out demons"? (Matt. 10:8)[17] The practice which one encounters particularly in the independent African churches as well as in the Coptic church of Egypt, namely, the ministry of healing, strongly fits the New Testament world and focuses attention upon one of the undoubtedly authentic facets of Jesus' own ministry facets which have again been discovered and experienced in a variety of cultural contexts.

17. G. Vermes, *Jesus the Jew* (London: Collins, 1973), pp. 58, 61.

The Jewish and the Christian Understanding of the New Testament

Without wishing to minimize the important contributions to a new understanding of Jesus which originate in other cultures, one has to say that it is particularly from the side of Jewish scholarship that very incisive questions are being put to those who, by way of their church missions, have brought and still attempt to bring Jesus to other cultures. This is partly true because Jews have "re-read" the New Testament itself in an often surprising way. But perhaps the most urgent Jewish questions come up where they concern the idea that Jesus is the messiah who has already come, that the kingdom of God has already dawned and that redemption has already been realized. Very often the church has regarded itself as the fulfillment of the kingdom of God or even equated itself with the kingdom of God. That faith in the messiah and the kingdom that had already come was the basis for a triumphalist interpretation and conduct toward people of other faiths. It was a dominating church which often brought a "colonial Christ" to other continents. Jesus' followers came rather to rule than to serve.

From the very first centuries, in their dialogues with Jews, Christians appealed to the Old Testament to "prove" that Jesus of Nazareth was the messiah promised in Scripture.[18] They thought this argument was reinforced by the fact that in the course of world history Christians had become powerful, whereas Jews had become powerless.[19]

R. R. Geis has pointed out the danger of the link with power which led to the imperial church of Constantine: "This feeds the fatal illusion that there can and has to be, in

18. H. J. Schoeps, *Israel und die Christenheit* (Munich and Frankfurt: Ner-Tamid Verlag, 1961), p. 33.
19. B. Knappert and H. Starck, *Umkehr und Erneuerung* (Neukirchen: Neukirchener Verlag, 1980), p. 140.

the literal sense, a Christian empire. From this illusion stem the bloody, never-ending wars of annihilation against unbelievers and heretics, and the grisly horrors of crusades and inquisition. By these means Christianity does not triumph over the world, but the pagan world triumphs over Christianity."[20] And that in turn led to a triumphalist understanding of the significance and role of Jesus Christ. C. Thoma correctly points out the danger of ideologizing messianic hope. "The Messiah-already-come served as pretext for triumphalist, imperialistic ideas in the church."[21]

This triumphalism of the church—this centuries-long alliance of the church with power and the understanding of Christ's rule in that light—provided a context for more than the transmission of the gospel. Crusades were conducted against Muslims, Jews could be persecuted, the sword and the cross could move side-by-side in the "Christianization" of Latin America and the Philippines. Jesus was again betrayed, denied, crucified among the Indians, Jews, and blacks.

From Jewish critics Christians can at least learn that some forms of "imperial" or absolutist Christology have to be given up.[22] Emil Fackenheim has stated that after Auschwitz Christians can no longer maintain that in Jesus Christ redemption has come.[23] That statement takes us back to the New Testament. As things stand, a Christian will never be able to follow a Jew in saying that Jesus was not the messiah, or that he was merely the forerunner of the messiah (Maimonides), without by that token denying the

20. R. R. Geis, *Unbekanntes Judentum* (Freiburg: Herder-Bücheri, 1961), pp. 231ff.

21. C. Thoma, *A Christian Theology of Judaism,* Helga Croner, trans. and ed. (New York: Paulist Press, 1980), pp. 63, 64.

22. Knappert and Starck, pp. 160, 165.

23. G. Baum, "De holocaust en de politieke theologie" *Concilium* 20 (Oct. 1984): 46.

Christian faith as it has come down to us in the New Testament. But a Christian can and must learn from Jewish critics that the coming of the messiah in which he or she believes cannot and may not be construed in triumphalist fashion. Definitive and total redemption has not yet been achieved—that much has to be said precisely on New Testament grounds.

In the past the church, not the least in its missionary outreach, has often placed a one-sided emphasis on the "already" dimension of the coming of the messiah, the kingdom, and redemption at the expense of the "not-yet" side of redemption and fulfillment. In the New Testament, by contrast, one finds a relationship full of tension between the idea that the messiah has come and that the kingdom has come near, *and* the prayer: "thy kingdom come," prayed in the shadow of the still-to-be expected coming or *parousia*.

Partly as a result of listening to Jewish voices, Christians are (again) beginning to realize that they do not know what the complete image of Jesus Christ is going to be. In this connection it is striking that from within African circles objections arose to the acceptance of an African Christological title like "chief" because it might occasion a similar triumphalist misunderstanding and imply the neglect of a *theologia crucis* in favor of a *theologia gloriae*.

Some time ago K. H. Kroon, speaking in the context of Jewish missions, remarked: "People say Jews must repent and turn. But if you ask them to what and to whom, they say: to Christ—as if that makes everything clear and as though we are speaking of a 'well-known figure.'"[24]

Jews can protect us from an all-too-facile notion that Christians already have a complete understanding of who Jesus is and in fact know him well. In the book of Revelation Jesus is referred to as "the Word of God." "He has a name

24. K. H. Kroon, *Blijvend verzet* (Zeist: Eltheto-NCSV, 1982), p. 87.

written on him that no one but he himself knows" (Rev. 19:12, NIV). The complete or ultimate name is evidently not yet known except to himself. For a Christian this passage contains a warning not to imagine that he or she already completely knows the name of Jesus. At the conclusion of the summary of the so-called "heroes of faith" which are reviewed in the eleventh chapter of the Letter to the Hebrews it is stated that "only together with us would they be made perfect" (11:40, NIV).

One wonders whether it cannot be said similarly that "we today" cannot grasp the complete knowledge of the mystery revealed to us in Jesus Christ—his present and future identity—apart from those who have come and will come after "us" from other cultures and religions.

C. JESUS CHRIST THE SAVIOR

An important Reformation adage, expressed in words attributed to Philip Melanchthon, has always been: "To know Christ is to know his benefits" *(Hoc est Christus cognoscere beneficia eius cognoscere).* In his 1545 Catechism, Calvin asks the following question about the treatment of Jesus' life in the Apostles' Creed: "Why do you leap at once from his birth to his death, passing over the whole history of his life?" The answer is, "Because nothing is treated of here but what so properly belongs to our salvation as in a manner to contain the substance of it."

For many of those who over the centuries dedicated themselves to "preaching Christ among the nations of the world" it was the transmission of precisely this knowledge which was central—and this was definitely not true only in the Herrnhut (Moravian) mission. In this understanding of the gospel—which is not just a post-Reformation phenomenon either—the core was a concern to preach reconciliation

The black Nazarene: "the Lord of Quiape"
This lifesize image of the black Nazarene, formally known as
Nuestro Padre Señor Jesus de Nazareno, was made of dark
hardwood by a baptized Aztec. In the seventeenth century it
was transported from Mexico to the Philippines, and it now
rests in the Quiapa church in Manila. On the ninth of January
men take turns carrying it in procession while bystanders
attempt to kiss its foot or touch its garments. The rest of the
year the image stands in a shrine inside the church and attracts
numerous pilgrims seeking salvation and healing. Devotees
swear by the miraculous power of the "Señor."

with God through the sacrifice of Christ on the cross. The soteriological significance of Jesus Christ was the crucial center—if not the whole. If this knowledge is not passed on people will be lost forever—this idea constituted an important motivation for much missionary activity.

In Spanish and Latin American Christology, which focused on the helpless child in his mother's arms and on the suffering bleeding victim of Golgotha, it is suggested that his infancy and death are emphasized because the two central truths of Christianity are the incarnation and the atonement. The "Spanish Christ" brought to Latin America is "the tragic Victim." "Bruised, corpse-like, bloodless, and blood-streaked images, twisted Christs that struggle with death, and recumbent Christs that have succumbed to it"— these are the images one finds, for instance, in a church in Santa Domingo, in Lima, Peru, called *El Señor del Sepulchro*, "The Lord of the Sepulchre."[25]

A similar sculpture can be found in Manila, the Philippines, a country Christianized by the same Spaniards, where in the church of Quiapo the "black Nazarene," a wooden image of Jesus, lies in a shrine. But this perspective is present in many other countries as well. R. W. Taylor, writing about Jesus in Indian art, says that leading painters tend to represent him in his suffering and depict very little of his life and teachings, and the latter only as they lead to his suffering.[26]

The Indian theologian Vengal Chakkarai links the dominance of this emphasis in Western churches with the fact that the Latin church has been pervaded by the practical, moral, and juridical genius of Rome and therefore tends

25. J. A. MacKay, *The Other Spanish Christ* (New York, 1932), pp. 96, 97, 114.

26. R. W. Taylor, *Jesus in Indian Paintings* (Madras: Christian Literature Society for India, 1975), p. 99.

to gravitate naturally toward the redemptive and legal aspects of the Lord's work.[27] However this may be, the fact is that in other representations of Jesus the focus is different, which is not to say that in the various new Latin American and Asiatic images the soteriological significance of Jesus or his messianic identity is denied. In this connection it is worthwhile to say that also in the New Testament there are different emphases, emphases that do not lie exclusively within the domain of soteriology.

According to John Mbiti, an African theologian, the soteriological significance of Jesus' death is a consequence or an effect, not the preceding assumption, of his death on the cross. The Aladura church, the church of the Lord, he says, has no interest in the suffering and death of Jesus as sacrifice.[28] According to Kofi Appiah-Kubi, in the eyes of Africans the Christ who acts as mediator before God, pleading the cause of guilty people and intervening in favor of sinners, has no appeal. In Africa there is a different notion of sin. Missionary instruction with regard to sin (the basis for traditional soteriology), says Kofi, is alien to the African mind and consequently out of order. The African attaches much value to social harmony, more than any teaching on sin.[29]

It is clear that, implicitly or explicitly, the images of Jesus created in other cultures and contexts confront the traditional Western approach with a question mark. It is again the Jewish voices which are the most pronounced at

27. V. Chakkarai, *Jesus the Avatara* (Madras: Christian Literature Society for India, 1930[2]), p. 72; *The Cross and Indian Thought* (Madras: Christian Literature Society for India, 1932).

28. J. S. Mbiti, "Some African Concepts of Christology," in G. F. Vicedom, ed., *Christ and the Younger Churches* (London: S.P.C.K., 1972), p. 54.

29. Kofi Appiah-Kubi, "Jesus Christ: Some Christological Aspects from African Perspectives" in J. S. Mbiti, ed., *African and Asian Contributions to Contemporary Theology* (Geneva: W.C.C. Ecumenical Institute, 1977), p. 57.

this point. Geza Vermes points out that three-fifths of the Nicene Creed (A.D. 325) "is concerned with the focus of this faith: Jesus the messiah." The resulting portrait of the Jesus of Christianity, in his view, shows "a total lack of proportion between history and theology, fact and interpretation." "In formulating her profession of faith, the church shows passionate interest in Christ's eternal pre-existence and glorious after-life but of his earthly career the faithful are told next to nothing, save that he was born and died."[30] In the same connection and spirit, Pinchas Lapide refers to a "three-days" Christology which in his opinion came in the place of a "thirty-years" Jesuology. All that is essential in Jesus' life and death tends to shrivel to the status of pre-history leading to his resurrection and ascension. According to the Creed, after all, Jesus barely lived. He hastened from cradle to cross and all he did and said is ignored—no Sermon on the Mount, no gospel of the kingdom, no healings. Did he, as Tertullian and Anselm say, come only to die? asks Lapide. Lapide believes that in this fashion no justice is done to his humanity or Jewishness.[31]

Latin American theologians of liberation also underscore this absence of interest in the historical Jesus—the actual course of his life, his fundamental life-choices, what he did and did not do. In the imagination and experience of many Christians, these theologians say, the actual historical life of Jesus, except for his birth and death, plays no role.

The urgent question to Christians is whether this emphasis should be the only concentration in their image of Jesus and must be so "transmitted" to others. The element in the contributions from Jewish scholars and those from other continents like Latin America which should be seri-

---

30. Vermes, p. 15.
31. P. Lapide, *Jeder kommt zum Vater; Barmen und die Folgen* (Neukirchen: Neukirchener Verlag, 1984), p. 24.

ously considered by Christians are their attention to the entire history of Jesus' life and not only to its outcome or "benefit." It is only when Christians pay attention to the whole of Jesus' life that his suffering and death and their meaning are seen in true perspective. The significance of Jesus' life cannot be derived only from the end, apart from the events of the preceding years.

As was remarked earlier, in the New Testament one finds several "Christologies" or ways in which the meaning of Jesus' life, person, and work are explained. The same is true of his death. H.-R. Weber, for instance, has stated that in the so-called *Logia*-source—a collection of words of Jesus to which New Testament scholars refer—Jesus' death is not yet interpreted soteriologically.[32] The passion narratives of Matthew, Mark, and Luke do not interpret Jesus' death, by reference to quotations from Scripture, as one of redemption or atonement. This is clear, for example, from Mark 15:27: "And with him they crucified two robbers, one on his right and one on his left," and from the Scripture "and (he) was numbered with the transgressors" (Isa. 53:12). It would appear that according to a very old tradition no strictly soteriological meaning was assigned to the death of Jesus. At that stage the expression "He died for our sins," one that played such a large role in the creed of the early church, was still absent. According to Weber, it was possible in a certain stage of the formation of tradition to confess one's faith in Jesus without referring to his death on the cross: "He was manifested in the flesh, vindicated in the Spirit, seen by angels, preached among the nations, believed on in the world, taken up in glory" (1 Tim. 3:16).[33]

What I mean to say in particular, therefore, is that Jesus

32. Cf. L. Schottroff and W. Stegemann, *Jesus von Nazareth; Hoffnung der Armen* (Stuttgart: Verlag W. Kohlhammer, 1978), p. 79.
33. Weber, pp. 34, 40, 50.

need not be understood and presented only and exclusively in terms of his suffering and death, his sacrifice on the cross. Such exclusivity can deprive a person of a sense of the life history of Jesus in its entirety, and that which happened in Holy Week (the *passio magna*), however important, comes to stand in stark isolation from that whole. By this process the true and complete humanity of Jesus is obscured, because the history of Jesus, the Jesus who existed in a concrete historical, societal, political, and religious context which helped to shape his decisions and perspective, is neglected. It is this point which is especially emphasized in black theology and the theology of liberation. Someone like Charles de Foucauld even viewed as extremely essential the thirty "hidden" years when Jesus lived in Nazareth, the years before his public ministry. Foucauld made it his business, during his years of mission in North Africa and elsewhere, particularly to live in harmony with those "hidden years" of Jesus.[34]

Pinchas Lapide poses the question: Cannot a comprehensive view of Jesus be a valuable contribution to a religious dialogue between his spiritual disciples and his physical brothers? Would not such a Christology, one that is faithful to Scripture and that revives the living one (Rev. 1:18)—as Jew, as rabbi, as preacher of the Sermon on the Mount, as a man of God—be an ecumenical contribution to a reconciliation which makes the Nazarene our peace (Eph. 2:14—"For he is our peace")?[35]

This is not to say that a Christian cannot, may not, or even must not speak about the soteriological significance of Jesus' ministry. The pivotal point is that to the minds of many Third-World theologians from Africa, Latin America, and

34. Denise Barrat and Robert Barrat, *Charles de Foucauld et la fraternité (Maitres Spirituels)* (Bourges: Editions du Sevil, 1958).
35. Lapide, p. 25.

Asia the significance of Jesus—his suffering and "work" "on
behalf of"—cannot be separated from the concrete historical
person who lived, labored, and was executed in a concrete
historical situation. Their concern is that his death not be
viewed without relating it to his entire life, together with its
concrete decisions and choices, this life of total self-invest-
ment on behalf of the poor, the oppressed, and the sinful. It
is *that* life which God confirmed—by the resurrection from
the dead by which he was constituted Son of God in power
(Rom. 1:4). By that event something new came into being, a
new impulse was given, a new future opened. That "story of
a living one" is the good news which is told and must be told
in every culture. From the time of the early church in the first
century and ever after in a variety of cultures, the experience
has been that in Jesus God appeared bringing salvation,
"decisive salvation," "salvation from God," the God "concerned with the love of man" (Schillebeeckx).

Jesus as Liberator?

For many Christians throughout the centuries the quintes-
sence of the gospel and the significance of Jesus consisted
in reconciliation and redemption. In addition to, and sometimes over against, this focus there is today a strong emphasis on the significance of Jesus and his message not only
for the personal and individual salvation of people but also
and particularly for the salvation and well-being of corporate man and creation. That is what comes to expression
in such terms as Jesus the Liberator, or Jesus Christ the
black messiah.

Centuries ago already Bartholomé de Las Casas recognized the Indians as scourged Christs and unmasked and
exposed their exploitation and untimely deaths. In this connection Gutiérrez raises the question whether one can claim
to be concerned over the eternal salvation of those who are

in danger of being lost and at the same time withdraw from (co-)responsibility for the injustice, hunger, and temporal misfortune of people in the world?[36] Very often today "the cry of the Poor" is played off against "the cry of the Lost." Las Casas, as we saw earlier, regarded the Indians more as the "Poor" than as the "Heathen" (or "Lost").[37]

Dom Helder Camara, the well-known bishop in Brazil, has stated that "in a world where two-thirds of the people are in a state of underdevelopment and hunger how can we squander huge sums on the construction of temples of stone, forgetting the living Christ who is present in the person of the poor? And when shall we come to understand that in too sumptuous churches the poor have not had the courage to enter and to feel at home? But Christ is there anyway, groveling in misery and hunger, living in ramshackle huts, without medical attention, without work, and without a future."[38]

The same thing is clearly articulated by Manas Buthelezi, a South African theologian: "Some remind us that all Christians 'meet at the foot of the cross of Calvary mountain'; they overlook the fact that if this is true Christians must also meet as human beings at the foot of Table Mountain in Cape Town in order to make laws and vote on matters that relate to the welfare of the body which is the temple of the Holy Spirit."[39]

In other words, these liberation theologians do not wish to ignore the significance of Jesus as Savior but do assert that this focus may not be abstracted from his signif-

36. G. Gutiérrez, *The Power of the Poor in History* (Maryknoll, NY: Orbis, 1983), p. 77.

37. Gutiérrez, p. 194.

38. Claus Bussmann, *Who Do You Say? Jesus Christ in Latin American Theology* (Maryknoll, NY: Orbis, 1985), pp. 75, 168.

39. Manas Buthelezi, "Daring to Live for Christ," in *Mission Trends, No. 3*, G. H. Anderson and T. F. Stransky, eds. (Grand Rapids: Eerdmans, 1976), p. 178.

icance for the social and political situations of oppression
and poverty. They have developed a sharper eye for the fact
that—to cite one example—deliverance from slavery in
Egypt, the house of bondage, is not only a "spiritual"
deliverance but also and very definitely a deliverance from
slavery. They are very sure that the issue there is the self-
arousal of a God who has observed, and does not tolerate,
the oppression under which the Israelites had to suffer.
"And God heard their groaning, and God remembered his
covenant with Abraham, with Isaac, and with Jacob" (Exod.
2:24).

Latin American theologians of liberation, as well as
African and Asiatic theologians, consistently point out the
inseparable connection between "redemption" and "liberation." Tissa Balasuriya, a theologian from Sri Lanka, makes
the point that Jesus never pulls apart the strands of personal,
religious, and social deliverance. In his opinion the social
teachings of Jesus have great relevance for today when a
whole civilization has been and is built on "individualism,
elitism, consumerism, and the ruthless exploitation of the
weak by the strong and of the poor by the strong and rich."
He points out that reflection on Christ's death and resurrection did not lead the Christian church to reform "the values
and structures of society." Instead, "even this central event
in Christ's life had rather an individualistic impact on persons. Early Christians had a messianic expectation of a new
kingdom; but to a high degree Christianity lost "this apocalyptic vision as well as the social dimension of its message." In Balasuriya's opinion, today "we need a return to
the original vision of Christ and of the early Christians." We
need to rethink Christian theology. He emphasizes as essential to this reorientation the rediscovery of Jesus of Nazareth
as a human person totally dedicated to the unselfish service
of his neighbor because God is love, and the rediscovery of
"the cosmic Christ as the expression of the universal plan of

God for the whole of humanity and the universe." "Thereby we can discover," says Tissa Balasuriya, "the contemporary and future dimensions of *Christ* who suffered and died for man's liberation and whose height and depth, length and breadth we must continually seek."[40]

By way of these African, Asiatic, and Latin American contributions we increasingly discover that Jesus did not just come for "sinners" but also and especially for "those sinned against" (Raymond Fung). Care will be needed to avoid polarization around the significance of Jesus' person and work so that "redemption" and "deliverance" are played against each other, a polarization between what is popularly called "evangelical" and "ecumenical" theology.

Perhaps a response from the African context can help us overcome this false dilemma. In this connection an African theologian, Malcolm McVeigh, mentions three streams flowing into the same reservoir.

One stream comes from missionary Christianity and identifies salvation as liberation from sin. Another stream comes from liberation theology cast in the Latin American mold, which understands salvation as liberation from oppressive political, social, and economic conditions. Still a third stream comes from traditional Africa and sees salvation as liberation from the objective forces of evil that lie behind sickness and misfortune and the daily tragedies of life.

Jesus was concerned about the forgiveness of sins but also about the healing of disease and the liberation of the poor and oppressed, to whom he brought the good news.[41]

40. Tissa Balasuriya, *Jesus Christ and Human Liberation,* Quest Series (1981; reprint, Colombo: Centre for Society and Religion), pp. 54, 72, 79, 91, 108.

41. Malcolm McVeigh, "Africa: The Understanding of Religion in African Christian Theologies," in *What is Religion? An Inquiry for Christian Theology,* Mircea Eliade and David Tracy, eds. (New York: Seabury, 1980), p. 60.

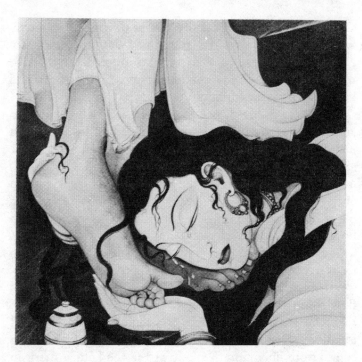

Mary Magdalene
This depiction is the work of the Indian painter Frank Wesley.

D. THE IMITATION OF CHRIST

"Christians believe in the cross, the Jews carry it," says Pinchas Lapide.[42] The second part of this statement has been true for innumerable Jews in a history of many centuries, and right into our own. There have also been millions of other "crossbearers" in the world and they still exist. The well-known French author Francois Mauriac, in his book *The Son of Man*, writes about this as follows:

> Simone Weil was obsessed all her life by the millions of slaves who were crucified before Christ was born, by the immense forest of gibbets upon which so many precursors were nailed and to whom no centurion rendered homage after having heard their last cry. For my part, I am much more obsessed by all the crosses that have been constantly erected after Christ—erected by a blind and deaf Christianity which never recognizes in the poor bodies it submits to questioning the Christ whose pierced hands and feet Christians kiss so piously on Good Friday. . . .
>
> To take only one example: Spain conquered the New World as a messenger of Christ and in order to evangelize it. Why then did she annihilate many peoples with the worst kind of ferocity: the kind inspired by motives of financial gain? Why does the history of the conquistadors not shock us more? And if I speak of Spain I am not forgetting the beam that is in my own eye as a Frenchman. There runs through Christian history, for all kinds of reasons, an attitude of invincible scorn toward less developed peoples. The historical relationship between dominating and dominated peoples has not changed appreciably since the time of Christ, even though, in the economic order, it has not worsened; this has happened to the extent that an increase of power brought to men by Christian liberation has been used to dominate those who did not receive the light. The natural riches of underdeveloped countries has, without

42. Lapide, p. 63.

their willing it, released a covetousness among Christian nations: a vice which, in attempting to glut itself, has spilled much blood. Their domination is perpetuated by methods which testify that it is not the imitation of Jesus Christ but the imitation of His executioners that has too often been the rule of the Christian West in the course of history. . . .

But whatever our reasons or excuses after nineteen centuries of Christianity, Christ never appears to modern executioners to be one with the criminal; the Holy Face never reveals itself in the countenance of the Arab which is forced to bear the marks of a commissioner's fist. How strange it is that they never think of their God tied to a column and delivered to the cohort, especially when it is a case of one of those dark faces with Semitic features; that they never hear His voice in the cries and supplications of their victim: "You do it to me." One day His voice will be heard, and it will no longer be suppliant. It will cry out to them and to all of us who have accepted and perhaps approved these things: "I was that young man who loved his country and fought for his king; I was that brother whom you forced to betray his brother." Why has this grace never been given to any baptized executioner? Why don't the soldiers of the modern cohort sometimes drop their whips and fall on their knees at the feet of the one they scourge?[43]

Just as Francois Mauriac did in our century, Bartholomé de Las Casas in the sixteenth century recognized the marks of the crucified Christ in those who were "scourged." He judged it to be a very real possibility that the Spaniards by their actions in Latin America, while claiming to seek the eternal salvation of the Indians, were in grave danger of forfeiting their own. The statements of both Mauriac and Las Casas constitute a warning to those who believe they can know Jesus without being his disciples in the concrete choices of life.

43. F. Mauriac, *The Son of Man* (New York: World Publishing Co., 1958), pp. 112-17.

And what does it mean that so many people—both before Christ (Simone Weil) and apart from the (historical) Jesus Christ—take his path without knowing him, at least in the confessional sense of the word. Aloysius Pieris addresses this problem by citing a statement by Fulton Sheen, who said: "The West is seeking a Christ without the cross while the East has a cross without Christ." Pieris does not consider this statement to be on target. "If there is no Christ without the cross, then can there be a cross without Christ? Can that which God has joined together ever be separated?"[44]

The only way to know Jesus as the truth is to follow his footsteps. This truth is "discovered," "encountered," or "revealed" by following his way. Evidently it is possible to take his road without (as yet) recognizing him. When the disciples learn that there are people casting out demons without following Jesus, Jesus answers: "He that is not against us is for us" (Mark 9:40). Of Moses it is said that he considered "abuse suffered for the Christ" greater wealth than the treasures of Egypt, for he looked to the reward (Heb. 11:26). The author of Hebrews obviously thought that Moses could be directly linked to Christ, although Moses did not know him and could not have known him in the literal, historical sense of the word.

In this connection J. B. Metz has referred to a "discipleship-Christology." Such a Christology does not express itself primarily in abstract concepts but in stories of discipleship. This Christology, says Metz, also opposes Christianity to the extent that it regards itself as a kind of triumphalist religion.[45] In other words, this Christology is at odds with the Constantine, Byzantine, Pantocratic (in the secular sense

44. Pieris, "Mission of the Local Church," p. 127. (Arrived at by reverse translation.—TRANS.)

45. J. B. Metz, "Met het oog op de joden; christelijke theologie na Auschwitz," *Concilium* 20 (Oct. 1984): 39. (The translation here is based on the Dutch text.—TRANS.)

of the word), and colonial images of Christ.[46] The questions which Metz then poses can be considered rhetorical: "Has not our discipleship become too much a spiritual discipleship, our love too much a spiritual love, our suffering a spiritual suffering, our exile a spiritual exile, persecution a spiritual persecution?"[47] And one could add this: our poverty too much a merely spiritual poverty? As we saw earlier, it was Tissa Balasuriya who pointed to the influence of *The Imitation of Christ,* attributed to Thomas à Kempis, which urged Asiatic Christians in the direction only of spiritual discipleship to the neglect of concrete discipleship in the sphere of politics and social life.[48] A similar remark has been made about the impact on missions in Asia and Africa of John Bunyan's *Pilgrim's Progress,* which also promoted a spiritualization of discipleship as well as of the biblical message.[49]

The churches, says Tissa Balasuriya, need to be evangelized by the world, for the world can reveal to the churches some of the broader implications of the gospel of Jesus Christ which they have either forgotten or never discovered.[50] In my opinion, we must carefully note both of these possibilities. The first one has repeatedly been stated and granted. As a result of the influence of Mahatma Gandhi, it has been said, Christians have learned to understand the Sermon on the Mount anew. That may be true, but it implies that Christians had forgotten it. Gandhi merely called Christians' attention to something they knew or had been in a position to know. But the second point which Tissa

46. K. Koyama, *Mount Fuji and Mount Sinai: A Pilgrimage in Theology* (London: SCM, 1984), p. 242.

47. Metz, p. 39.

48. See chapter V, part 1.

49. Cf. G. Verstraelen-Gilhuis, *From Dutch Mission Church to Reformed Church in Zambia* (Franeker: T. Wever, 1982).

50. Balasuriya, p. 119.

Balasuriya makes is as important if not more so: new dis-
coveries are made, so that it can be said, "We did not know
that, nor could we have known."

The Letter to the Hebrews begins by stating that "in
many and various ways God spoke of old to our fathers by
the prophets; but in these last days he has spoken to us by
a Son" (Heb. 1:1-2). This statement has often been interpreted as if it meant that now—in an unequivocal way—
the last word about Jesus Christ has been spoken. Is it not
more likely to mean that one can, must, and will also speak
about the revelation of the Son in many and various ways
and that this process of understanding and discovery is not
yet complete?

Karl Rahner says that explicit Christianity, as it has
become manifest in the form of the present church, has itself
not yet attained its definitive form as long as the anonymity
of the others continues. Only when the fullness of the Gentiles, with their very distinct religious experiences and traditions, has made its contribution to the historic shape of the
Christian community can the opposition to Christ and his
church disappear. To that extent it is the church itself which,
in its relation to non-Christians, is also changeable and
needs completion.[51]

"As it is, we do not yet see everything in subjection to
him. But we see Jesus, who for a little while was made lower
than the angels, crowned with glory and honor because of
the suffering of death, so that by the grace of God he might
taste death for every one" (Heb. 2:8, 9).

We see Jesus—but not or no longer as a worldly conqueror, as though his kingdom were of this world, in a
triumphalism that has (already!) been claimed with respect

---

51. K. Rahner, "Christianity and the Non-Christian Religions," in
Church and History, vol. 5 of *Theological Investigations,* Cornelius Ernst,
trans. (Baltimore: Helicon, 1966), pp. 115-34.

to the Jews and was rudely asserted in the face of Muslims in the crusades. Such a view and such an understanding becomes impossible if we see Jesus, as Hebrews does, as one to whom everything is not yet in subjection, who in his suffering was made lower than the angels, and who still suffers—in agony till the end of the world (Pascal)—with the least of his brothers and sisters.

This is clear: Jesus Christ cannot and may not be bound to one specific context, Western or Eastern. Responses to him have come and will continue to come from a great many different contexts.

It is only at the end of all times that we shall be rooted and grounded in love and have power to comprehend together with all the saints—from Asia, Africa, the Americas, and Europe—what is the breadth and length and height and depth, and to know the love of Christ which surpasses knowledge (Eph. 3:18, 19).

INDEX OF NAMES

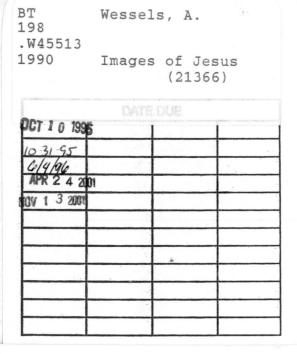